Native Soul

Unlocking Your Life's Potential

J Douglas Bottorff

Also by the Author

A Practical Guide to Meditation and Prayer

A Practical Guide to Prosperous Living

The Whisper of Pialigos

Native Soul

Unlocking Your Life's Potential

J Douglas Bottorff

UNITY®
Books

Unity Village, MO 64065-0001

Native Soul

First Edition 2011

$\mathcal{9}\backslash \iota\iota$

Unity Books titles are available at special discounts for bulk purchases for study groups, book clubs, sales promotions, book signings or fundraising. To place an order, call the Unity Customer Care Department at 1-866-236-3571 or email *wholesalesaleaccts @unityonline.org*.

Bible quotations are from the New Revised Standard version unless otherwise noted.

Cover design: Doug Brown

Interior design: The Covington Group, Kansas City, Missouri

Library of Congress Control Number: 2010943072

ISBN: 978-0-87159-352-8

Canada BN 13252 0933 RT

Special thanks to Anita Feuker, who reviewed this manuscript in its early stages and offered many helpful suggestions for greater clarity and simplicity.

Contents

Introduction

I have written this book specifically for the advanced student, though not in the sense the term *advanced* is usually employed. For me, the advanced student is one who has reached the realization that getting what you want from life involves waking up to what you are as a spiritual being. There are many who see their spiritual awakening as the means of acquiring things and conditions that will make them something more than they are now. In this book, I treat the spiritual awakening not as a means to an end but as an end in itself. Achieving this end, which is now and has always been within the reach of all, is the true starting place for getting what you want from life.

More than three decades' work as a minister has given me the opportunity to observe many people operating within a wide range of spiritual understanding. I think it is fair to say that when most start their studies of spiritual principles, their intention is to *get more out of life*. They feel that something is missing, that their previous attempts to fill the gaps haven't worked, and that the spiritual approach offers the surest way to get back on track in making their life a more fulfilling endeavor. And so it does.

I have also observed that many who have been on the spiritual path for years often express levels of frustration similar to those levels that originally prompted their search. They have obtained many new ideas, but they feel no closer to the satisfaction they crave. I suggest that this happens because they have adopted two commonly held erroneous beliefs. The first is that their current dissatisfaction is attributable to their limited understanding of God, that eventually they will gain enough understanding to give them the satisfaction they seek. The second belief is that in their present state they are spiritually incomplete, that they need to develop spiritually before they can reach a satisfying level of experience. Both assumptions are false.

If you are among these individuals, you now possess of all the knowledge you need to have a firsthand, personal relationship with your Creator/Sustainer. Furthermore, you are as complete now at your spiritual core as you will ever be. No natural barriers exist between your current self-perception and your completed soul. The only chasm that stands between where you are and where you want to be is a perceptual error. As long as you hold this perception of distance and separation from your spiritual home, you will continue to wander in a far and foreign country. The moment you drop this perception, you return to the warm reception of your spiritual home. Embracing the simple truth that you already have what you seek spiritually will revolutionize your approach to getting what you want from your spiritual quest and, in the broadest and most fulfilling sense, getting what you want from life.

Nearly all self-help literature is geared toward achieving the ideal person you dream of becoming. This book, taking the spiritual point of view, challenges such a notion and, more important, urges you to examine closely your beliefs about your own spiritual awakening. The ideas set forth here will help you open your mind to your *native soul*, that eternal dimension of you that is firmly established in the field of limitless energy we call God, the *Creative Life Force*. The traditional view of the *soul* is that it is in a state of evolving to a higher level. In this book, I counter that assumption with the recurrent theme: God will not and cannot give you any more than you already have. Your native soul is now complete and nothing is keeping you from experiencing your completeness.

The practice of meditation—periods of deliberate spiritual receptivity—is the narrow gate (Mt. 7:13-14) by which you enter the domain of your native soul. If you are meditating yet failing to experience your spiritual essence, you are not meditating, you are *thinking*. Meditation is the act of opening your intuitive portal, a faculty that enables you to experience the spiritual domain, to the living presence of your completed soul. Becoming successful at meditation does not require years of training, for there is actually very little to learn. Meditation is a receptive state that opens your awareness to the perpetual radiation of your soul. You already know how to receive spiritual light, and you have been doing so all along, though perhaps unconsciously. You invite the perpetual light of your soul into your field of awareness by assuming this simple attitude:

My completed soul is now radiating light.
I am conscious of this light.

When I mention meditation in this book, I am referring to a practice of internal reflection. You will want to spend quality time away from all distractions and enter a spiritually receptive state. This practice is your primary resource for tapping your inner power. However, you will also gain much by getting in the habit of experiencing the light of your soul while driving your car, shopping, conversing with people or taking a solitary walk. Bring this awareness into every aspect of your life. Given even a small chance, the light of your native soul will break forth, first as a small and seemingly insignificant thrill of energy. Return often to this experience and this tiny thrill becomes the steadfast beacon that will guide your every thought. You do not want to spend a mere percentage of your time in meditation; you want to spend *all* your time experiencing your life from your spiritual depths.

Do not think of meditation as a difficult practice you *must* adopt. Think of it instead as the birthing process for an entirely new vision. Emma Curtis Hopkins pointed out that "it is primarily what we most see [our inner vision], and not what we most think, that constitutes our presence, power and history" (2). Many people attempt to change their lives by changing their thinking. Your thinking follows your vision. The practice of meditation raises your vision and your thinking naturally conforms. All your executive faculties—faith, imagination, judgment, will and elimination—fall in line with the radiance of your soul. Take to heart the reminder Jesus gave to his listeners: "It is written in the prophets, 'And they shall all be taught by God'" (Jn. 6:45).

This book is a presentation of ideas that are based on my experience and understanding of the spiritual awakening. It is my prayer that these ideas touch you in ways that make a significant difference in the way in which you perceive yourself, and that this shift in perception is enough to set you on a true and genuine path toward getting what you want from life.

– 1 –

Fulfillment Is Closer Than You Think

Imagine for a moment that today is your day to die.

You're walking down the sidewalk and notice a 75 percent off sign at Macy's across the street. Excited, you dash forward, forgetting an important lesson your mother tried to teach you: *look both ways before crossing*. There is a big *thump*, but focused on the giant red and yellow SALE SALE SALE banner ahead, you give it no thought. But then something strange happens. You are no longer running across the street, you are hovering above it! You look down and see a body crumpled in front of a car, and you are surprised that it is *your* body! You are confused: it looks quite lifeless, but you feel very much alive. People start to gather and one man kneels next to your body and feels for a pulse. He announces that he thinks you are dead and a gasp ripples through the growing audience. You laugh to yourself and begin explaining that you are not dead, that you are quite well. The crowd pays no attention to you.

To add to your frustration, you begin to hear an unpleasant buzz and then you are traveling at great speed through a tunnel. You emerge into an atmosphere of light more beautiful than any you have ever seen. By now you are growing accustomed to the fact that you are not in your physical body. You quickly adapt to your new environment and to the fact that you are now completely unencumbered by time and space. You have a body, not of flesh and bone but energy, which you can move at the incredible speed of thought. Your senses of vision and hearing are absolutely acute. Your mind is crisp and fluent with universal wisdom. All the so-called knowledge that you have accumulated through your entire life pales in significance to this universal wisdom that is so seamlessly and effortlessly integrated into your very essence. For the first time in your life you have no questions. You are a *knower* of the Real, so completely immersed in unconditional love that you feel overwhelming love for everyone and everything. You can't help yourself. Your former efforts to love seem completely inadequate in comparison to this majestic atmosphere of love that completely permeates your being.

At this point you realize you are in the presence of a Being of Light so beautiful, so loving that you can only feel awe. This Being begins showing you a three-dimensional screening of every detail of every event in your life. You see all the wonderful things you did and all the not-so-wonderful things too. The Being sees all too, but remains completely loving, supportive and nonjudgmental. When the review is over, the Being asks if you are happy with what you have seen or do you think you could do better? You know you can do better because you have gained such a wonderful perspective of the boundless nature of your essence, your spiritual identity. You want only to remain in the light, yet something of your life in the physical body—the image of a spouse or other family members who would benefit from your continued influence—beckons. In the next instant, you are aware that you are in an ambulance being rushed to the hospital. Your stirring startles the paramedic, who clearly thought you were dead.

According to those who have had a near-death experience, these are just a few of the conditions that you and I, free from our physical bodies, may experience. Such reports are not only fascinating, they also challenge many of our commonly held religious and scientific beliefs about who and what we are and what possible meaning life on this planet might have. We can become so enamored with visions of a spectacular afterlife that we may fail to see how research into the near-death experience applies to life in the here-and-now. The connection is so simple that it is not immediately apparent. The profound reality revealed by these experiences is the invincibility of the person who has supposedly died. The inescapable implication is that this condition exists *now*, that every individual inhabiting a physical body is ultimately indestructible.

The Goal of Fulfillment

Regardless of specifics, getting what you want from life involves obtaining fulfillment in all your endeavors. This is true whether you seek the acquisition of more money, connecting with the right partner, moving into a new career, planning a family vacation or deepening your spiritual awareness. It is worth noting that nearly all people who momentarily step out of their bodies report a level of satisfaction and fulfillment so complete that they, like the world's great spiritual teachers, are forced to speak in similes, metaphors and even parables in an effort to explain the depth of their satisfaction. There are simply no words in our present vocabulary to adequately address the level of satisfaction they attempt to describe.

From these accounts emerge two critical pieces of information. First, *the ability to experience this indescribable level of satisfaction not only exists in you right now, it is also your very essence.* In this book, I refer to this essence as your *native soul*. Christian-based New Thought literature designates this core identity as *the Christ*, relating to Jesus and his discovery and expression of his own God-potential. The challenge of using this ancient term lies in the preconditioning and the misconceptions most of us carry about Jesus. We have made him into a larger-than-life personality, placing him at a level of spiritual development that is essentially unattainable. In contrast to this image, Jesus himself indicated that "the one who believes in me will also do the works that I do and, in fact, will do greater works than these" (Jn. 14:12).

To get the most from the teachings of Jesus, I assume he was speaking of accomplishments that are presently within my reach. The "me" he refers to is not him personally, but his spiritual core, his native soul. It is the same inner spiritual dimension that, as near-death research suggests, is fully developed, present and native to everyone, even those living the most average of lives. Jesus is saying that when you come to know and believe in your native soul, you can do the type of things he does and more. As one who is interested in a spiritual approach to getting what I truly want from life, I pay attention to this statement. Jesus becomes a relevant instructor, one who actually assists me in becoming conscious of my essential core, my native soul, the source of the genuine level of satisfaction that I seek.

The second critical piece of information that we can draw from these near-death accounts is this: It is clear from their sincere expressions of absolute joy that *material things are not needed to produce the deep fulfillment and gratification for which you yearn.* The sincere joy reported by near-death survivors completely contradicts the commonly held belief that accomplishments and material acquisitions are a primary source of fulfillment.

They suddenly find themselves in a state of having absolutely *nothing*, not even a body, and yet they report touching something so meaningful, so gratifying that they cannot adequately put it in words.

This does not mean that you are to discontinue or discount material pursuits and interests. The spiritual awakening enables you to see that the material level is but the surface aspect of a single continuum whose source begins in the invisible and whose expression is the visible. You gain the understanding that the material realm is intended to clothe you with symbols reflecting the joy, health, freedom, peace and abundance that naturally arise from within your spiritual depths.

You might think you have to study and meditate for years before attaining this level of understanding. Many near-death experiencers, however, say they learn more about themselves in the minutes they are out of the body than they have learned in all the years of living their earthly lives. Virtually all proclaim their near-death experience (which might aptly be renamed a near-life experience) as the most profoundly satisfying and educational event of their lives. In the blink of an eye, this experience jolts them into the awareness that they are a soul with a body, not a body that houses some vague and mysterious concept that has been dubbed a soul. As one woman reported:

> I was more conscious of my mind at the time than of that physical body. The mind was the most important part, instead of the shape of the body. And before, all my life, it had been exactly reversed. The body was my main interest and what was going on in my mind, well, it was just going on, and that's all. But after this happened, my mind was the main point of attraction, and the body was second—it was only something to encase my mind. I didn't care if I had a body or not. It didn't matter because

for all I cared my mind was what was important. (Moody 91)

Nothing New Is Acquired

It's important to note that the near-death experiencer did not suddenly acquire a new set of faculties or mental capabilities. The experience has the effect of peeling back, in a matter of moments, the varnish of a lifetime's false and misdirected beliefs. Beneath this veneer the native soul is absolutely complete, whole and immortal. These people describe communication by pure thought, faculties of sight and hearing that are pristine and superbly acute, and a mind that is sharp, able to retain and utilize staggering amounts of knowledge. They speak of pain-free bodies that are vitally charged and mobile as a bolt of lightning. They experience nothing resembling death or negation and realize that their souls are not dependent on or restricted to the physical body. Often they report awakening with a deep sense of purpose and connection within a much larger, universal context.

Perhaps the most amazing revelation is that their souls have not been harmed or diminished by their worst sins, their darkest moments of ignorance, or their most negative and self-destructive thinking. Yes, some report remorse for having lived meaningless, self-indulgent lives, and they express sadness for any harm they might have inflicted on others. They feel that had they known of this interior dimension they would not have made choices that were harmful to themselves and others. Even so, their negative actions did nothing to mar the shimmering jewel of their soul—a stark contrast to commonly held religious beliefs.

The "Soul-Bearing" Mechanism

These reports challenge established religious ideas. They also directly oppose the operational model of medical science that treats the individual as a product of electrical and chemical processes of the brain. According to this brain-based model, the death of the brain makes any further experience impossible. There are those within the scientific community, however, who do not agree.

The late Dr. Ian Stevenson, a pioneering researcher into cases of children who claim past life memories, went so far as to coin a term—*psychophore* (Greek: "soul bearing")—to name the possible mechanism that keeps the bodiless soul intact. We can draw an analogy to this mechanism from the field of information technology. I am writing this book on a laptop computer. The text is stored electronically on a hard drive. When I send it to my publisher, they will convert the electronic text into the material form of a book. It is now possible to email this entire manuscript. Because my computer transmits information without the use of physical wiring, there are moments when the text becomes a *disembodied* package of energy that flies through the air, passing through normal material barriers such as walls as easily as if they do not exist. You can throw a physical book through the air, but it will not pass through walls. Nor can you throw it very far. In the book's disembodied form, physical obstacles become irrelevant, and yet even when it is sent around the world, not a single word is lost in the transmission.

In this book I accept as a given, as do virtually all the world's religions, the soul's ability to exist apart from the body. Though the body provides a physical medium through which the effects of the soul are seen and expressed (as a book is expressed in paper or on a screen), the soul's ability to remain intact, like an

7

electronic manuscript, is not dependent on the physical medium of brain and body. The soul is, of course, much more complex than the electronic package that constitutes a manuscript, but the illustration is relevant as a model.

Your Soul Is Not Frail

Some on the spiritual path make the mistake of thinking that the soul is frail, that major repairs need to be made before they can even begin thinking about getting what they want from life. It is the perception of the soul rather than the soul itself that is in need of repair. In his parable of the stronger man, Jesus illustrated that the soul endures as the strongest aspect of our being:

> When a strong man, fully armed, guards his castle, his property is safe. But when one stronger than he attacks him and overpowers him, he takes away his armor in which he trusted, and divides his plunder. (Lk. 11:21-22)

Because this parable is cast in a rather violent tone, it is easy to miss its significance. The *strong man* is your senses-based identity. The *one stronger* is your native soul. Many make the mistake of thinking that, because it is so overpowering, the force behind random mental chatter is the strongest. The strongest, however, is that which is left standing when everything else, including your body, falls away. No matter how far you have wandered from your immortal essence, or how deeply engrossed you have become in pointless mental chatter, you have in no way marred or diminished your soul's strength and wholeness.

You Have Already Received

To get what you want from life you must start with this picture of completeness and dare to embrace it with the understanding of *what you are right now*. When Jesus instructed his followers to pray as if they had already received what they asked for (Mk. 11:24), he was pointing to this important insight. Material things are but symbols of spiritual realities. What you seek from material things is the experience of a deeper reality. You want love, so you seek a loving relationship. You want power, so you seek a position of power. You want more life, so you book a vacation. You want to increase your intelligence, so you sign up for some classes. While there may be plenty of things standing between you and the material good you have named, there is nothing standing between you and the reality you wish to experience. Allowing yourself to go within and experience the eternally accessible essence of what you seek, you draw to yourself the people and conditions reflective of this deeper reality. This is the principle taught by Jesus of seeking first the kingdom of God, and these things (the material counterpart) will be given as well (Mt. 6:33).

You cannot align with this principle if you believe you will receive the good you seek someday. Have you pored over ancient scripture, devoured all the latest spiritual best-sellers, trotted from teacher to ashram to temple to church? Have you turned over rocks in every corner of the material realm with the hope of finding the spiritual reality you desire? If so, you have fallen into a trap that snares many on the spiritual path. Getting what you want out of life begins with affirming that *you are already in possession of what you seek.*

In another example, suppose you feel the need for spiritual guidance. *Asking* for guidance reflects the belief that guidance

9

will commence as soon as you affirm it enough or evolve to a higher state of consciousness. Instead, embrace the truth that you are *now* being guided. You have never once been without guidance. Asking for guidance is, as H. Emilie Cady suggested, like affirming that the sun shines: "The sun shines because it is a law of its being to shine, and it cannot help it" (43). Regardless of how positive or negative you are, the sun *will* shine. Accept guidance with the same faith and understanding you have toward the dawning of a new day, and you will begin immediately to see evidence of what you seek.

You Have Already Set a Precedent

Does the process of opening your mind to a self-sustaining state of being sound a little uncertain? Think of a time when you cowered in the face of a crisis. You felt powerless. At some point, however, you said, "Enough! I have trembled in fear thus far, but I will tremble no longer." In that decisive moment, you remembered you were not given a spirit of fear but an invincible spirit of strength and courage, and that spirit suddenly broke forth like a hot beam of sunlight after days spent shivering beneath the cold clouds of fear. Even in the darkest moments the sun never left. Its power remained constant, undiminished.

This spiritual power has always been and will always be with you. It cannot be diminished by even the darkest clouds of ignorance that have kept you in the cold. In an instant the golden ray of spiritual power can burst through and change everything. The thing that had you shrinking in fear suddenly scurries away at the commands you issue from your newly reclaimed strength.

Spiritual power is not a force that enables you to overthrow negative conditions. Spiritual power gives you the insight needed to transcend negative appearances. It manifests through you as mental, emotional and physical strength. A perception of weakness is created when you are misaligned with your spiritual center. You see the negative condition as a force you have to overcome, so you ask God for more power. Because power is one of the fundamental attributes of your native soul, you need not ask for more. You need only remember that you have all the power required to rise above your fear of appearances.

An affirmation of power is the *action* of aligning your thought with that aspect of yourself already grounded in omnipotence. This alignment changes the way you see and interpret the negative condition, influences the way you interact with the condition, and ultimately changes the condition itself. Your objective is to shift your thinking to your unrestricted core, that inner point of power that is not subject to conditions. Success in working out every problem begins when you consciously connect with such aspects of your wholeness.

The Lost Pencil

There is a very different mindset between looking for something you own but have misplaced and looking for something you are not sure you have. Imagine you are using a pencil to write a note and your cell phone rings. You answer the call, talk a few minutes and then hang up. When you resume your writing task you cannot find your pencil. You know you had it and your partially finished note is proof. Determined to find it, you know it has to be somewhere near. A search is begun. Under the papers? No. On the floor? No. Under the printer?

No. In the wastebasket? No. Top drawer? No. It was here two minutes ago! Shirt pocket? No. Then, running your hands through your hair in frustration, you find the pencil behind your ear.

If, on the other hand, you decide to write a note and start looking through drawers for a pencil you're not sure is there, you will not give your search the same attention. Top drawer. No pencil drawer. No. You quickly conclude there isn't a pencil here, sigh and give up.

Jesus illustrated the same idea using the example of a woman who had 10 silver coins. Finding only nine in her purse, she lit a lamp and swept her house clean until she found the 10th (Lk. 15:8). This search was not based on speculation or blind faith. Her action was based on precise knowledge of exactly what was missing from her cache of coins.

Like this woman, you are endowed with definite knowledge that something is missing and that your life will be better if you find this missing piece. If you think of your native soul as something you already have and you've just forgotten that you have it, you will approach finding it very differently than if you think of it as something that will require years to cultivate. You look at your personal identity and it seems there is much to be done. This is due to how you view your soul and your personality. In the next chapter, we will explore the role of personality and the surprising part it plays in your soul's expression. Keep an open mind and heart. Fulfillment is closer than you think.

The Personality Factor

Some, having come to realize that their consciousness is structured around misleading senses-based information, conclude that their personality, their surface identity that they show the world, is a hindrance, a barrier between where they are and where they want to be in life. Many people, having reached the realization that most restrictions have been imposed by a personality void of spiritual understanding, come to regard the personality and the soul almost as polar opposites. The soul is good and in need of development, while the personality is a thing to be overcome, perhaps even discarded.

In her classic work *What Are You?* Unity author Imelda Octavia Shanklin explains why living strictly from the personal level is so unsatisfying:

> When you identify yourself solely with the personal you are not satisfied. There is a lack for which you cannot account, but which is very real to you. If you should voice your feeling you perhaps would say, "I want something. I do not know what it is that I want, but when I receive what I want I shall be satisfied." Knowing the personal, only, you have but superficial knowledge of yourself. Beneath the

surface the rich deeps of life summon you with overmastering appeal. Not knowing how to respond, you have a sense of confusion and restlessness. (7)

The personality indeed becomes a restricting factor when you see it as the sum of your being. A goldfish raised in a small fishbowl, for example, is perfectly content with its limited environment because it knows nothing different. Place a wild trout in that same bowl and it will jump out because it knows a world beyond those restricting glass walls. Like the trout, you feel restricted because you have attempted to stuff your limitless soul into a tiny senses-based personality that cannot possibly contain all that you are and certainly cannot give you all that you are trying to get from life. In your acquisitive quest you are continually plagued by restlessness and dissatisfaction. This discontentment, however, is simply the prompting of your native soul perpetually calling to you from its completed state of wholeness. It stands at the door of your senses-based personality and knocks, waiting patiently for you to open yourself to its larger world. Some, having come to realize the shortcomings of this fishbowl personality, respond with a form of self-denial, possibly self-loathing. They conclude that in order to get what they really want from life they will have to greatly restrict or eradicate the influence of the personality altogether.

A Function of the Soul

Of course, there are issues associated with the personality that prove to hinder our ability to get what we want from life. It is important that we explore some of these issues. Before we do, I want to say that, when properly understood, the personality itself is not a hindrance to be overcome. It is actually an important *function* of the soul. It allows you to *personalize* and communicate at the material level the universal energy that rises from your depths. When you deny or condemn your personality, you actually stymie your ability to express life·*on earth as it is in heaven* (Mt. 6:10). The personality is your outlet, the avenue through which you manifest the innate qualities of your native soul. When you hold a dim view of the role of personality, you are saying there is a part of you that is broken, and you will not be spiritually whole until you fix or dispose of it. As we have seen, you are already spiritually whole and, try as you may, you will never eliminate your personality. Nor do you want to.

A contributing factor to the negative view of the personality is a subtle misunderstanding of the derivation of the word itself. *Personality* comes from Latin, *persona*, whose original meaning was associated with the actor's mask. When you begin to make a distinction between your surface, senses-based identity and your spiritual identity, you are likely to think of the personality as a mask that hides your more substantial being, a barrier that keeps you from getting what you want from life.

The word *persona* was indeed associated with the actor's mask, but this association carried quite a different meaning than many have assumed. The mask was the vehicle for representing or presenting character. When the audience saw the mask, they would not see it as a shield behind which the actor was hiding. They would see the character the mask represented. An actor wearing a bear mask, for example, would be thought of by the audience as a bear. This is very different than using the mask to disguise and deceive, like a bank robber. The theatrical audience knew the mask was intended to convey the *real essence* of a given character. Nothing associated with deception was intended.

Even today, with the assistance of makeup, film technique and setting, a good actor puts on the mask of his or her character, not to deceive you into believing he or she is someone they are not, but to tell a story. The motive is healthy and the actor's mask is appropriate for its intended purpose. After all, we want to see great lovers, kings, queens, brilliant scientists and gallant warriors on our big screens, not the residents of Beverly Hills. For that we can turn to the personality-hungry tabloids that line the checkout lanes of our grocery stores.

The Profile in Cyberspace

We see many expressions of personality, some of which are contentious, abrasive and otherwise problematic. When understood in its spiritual context, however, the personality is an important component to the expression of your *whole* being, the medium through which you project the essence of your native soul into the three-dimensional world.

Think of the function of personality in this way: If you want to enter and utilize the many advantages of cyberspace, you must have an online identity. You create a profile that includes a screen name and other information you wish to share. This identity becomes your point of contact, your link for communication with anyone that has access to the Internet. You can then join a social network, order products, send pictures, play games or further your education.

The personality, as a function, serves exactly the same purpose. Just as your screen name and profile work as a communication *interface* between you and cyberspace, so your personality serves as an interface between you, an invisible spiritual being, and your material environment. We see a graphic illustration of the role of the personality interface when a person dies. Near-death research provides compelling evidence that even when the brain ceases to function, individual consciousness remains intact. What is lost is the personality interface, which includes the body and all that is communicated through the body. The severance of the interface makes communication with the physically deceased virtually impossible to any but the most psychically sensitive. As seen in the following example, this severing of communication is often a surprise and a source of frustration expressed by many near-death experiencers:

> The doctors and nurses were pounding on my body to try to get IV's started and to get me back, and I kept trying to tell them, "Leave me alone. All I want is to be left alone. Quit pounding on me." But they didn't hear me. So I tried to move their hands to keep them from beating on my body, but nothing would happen. I couldn't get anywhere. (Moody 44)

In this case, the personality interface has been temporarily disconnected. The doctors, unable to get a response, keep trying to reboot the personality. The patient, who is still very much alive, though unable to communicate, finds this aspect of their experience frustrating.

If you close your online account and delete your virtual personality, you continue to carry on your life. The difference is simply that you no longer maintain a presence in that cyber community. You may even join another online community that is more in keeping with your changing interests. Though the mentally healthy person does not confuse their online persona with who they are, most of us do make the mistake of thinking our body-based personality, in all its complexity, represents the

sum of our identity. Those who hold this view have so identi-
fied with their various idiosyncrasies, bodily characteristics
and social roles that they equate losing the personality interface
with the end of life.

The Earth-Centered Universe

It is true that our history of sensory input, from birth to the
present, explains much of our behavior. The combination of
genetics, gender, age, race, education, culture and a lifetime of
experience make a pretty good case for summarizing a person's
essence based on their mental and physical aspects alone. Our
exploration of the spiritual aspect of our being, however, raises
issues that force us to look beyond personality for our truly
defining attributes.

For those who think of personality as the defining essence of
the individual, it may be helpful to recall a time when conven-
tional wisdom held that the sun, the planets and the stars
revolved around the earth. The earth was seen as the defining
essence of the universe. Over time this view was revised by the
understanding that the earth revolves around the sun. Later,
astronomers began to see that our solar system rests in the arms
of the great spiral galaxy we know as the Milky Way. Today it
is common knowledge that the Milky Way is but one member
of the Local Group, a cluster of more than 35 galaxies with a
gravitational center located somewhere between the Milky Way
and Andromeda galaxies.

The same can and will be said of the personality-centered,
brain-based model of the individual. Until fairly recent times, if
you awakened from surgery and reported watching from a
corner of the ceiling your doctors operate on your body, or
if you tried to explain that you had just traveled through

something like a tunnel and met a being of light that touched you deeply with love and understanding, you might be a candidate for a psychiatric review. Fortunately many medical professionals are now taking the near-death experience and all its implications of a self-sustaining soul, including its ability to reincarnate, quite seriously. As the evidence mounts, science will confirm in the laboratory what the mystics long ago discovered in the cloistered cell and the desert caves: Consciousness transcends the physical and has the capacity to function independent of the brain. The native soul, not the personality, is the defining essence of the individual. The personality, however, plays an important role of expressing what we are.

A Lesson From the Iceberg

When it comes to understanding the human being, personality is but the proverbial tip of the iceberg. An iceberg is a single block of ice that exists simultaneously in two completely different realms. The visible part that extends into the air and sky represents about 10 percent of the berg's entire size. The remaining 90 percent extends into a completely different environment beneath the surface of the sea.

Like the iceberg, you exist simultaneously in two complementary yet completely different worlds. The bulk of your being is spiritual, unseen beneath the surface, but you project into the material environment a presence and distinct influence. The visible part of you, your body and the psychological functions displayed through your personality, represent the smaller exposed tip of your being. The body and personality provide the interface that enables complete interaction between the spiritual and material realms. Because most of us spend 90 percent of our time and energy addressing the needs and desires of the exposed 10 percent, we are either unaware or only vaguely aware of the other 90 percent. Because the senses-based identity dominates our attention, most of our quest for understanding arises from this superficial level. The time comes when we see that the most effective way to get what we want from life is to bring the 10 percent, the personality, into alignment with the larger 90 percent.

Image Is Everything

The problem with personality is that it has been thought of as the substance of the individual rather than as a function of the soul. This attitude was summed up in the slogan of an advertising campaign conducted by a popular camera manufacturer in the 80s: *Image is everything.* Advertisers, acutely aware of our propensity for buying images rather than products, earn billions of dollars a year creating product images that inspire feelings of good will, security and increased popularity through whiter teeth, faster cars, glossier hair, and, of course, more sparkling, attention-getting personalities.

You, too, may have adopted a similar approach to packaging yourself, placing approval from others ahead of how you actually feel about yourself. It's the way to get ahead in life, or so you were told. If your concern about what others think of you takes precedence over what you think of yourself, you may develop an attractive personality while feeling hollow and disjointed inside. As Jesus asked, What good is it if you gain the world but lose your soul? (Mk. 8:36).

The time comes when the effort of sustaining the "right" image becomes overwhelming. Projecting a personality of someone you are not might get you to the next checkpoint on your list of must-haves, but it will never give you the peace and true self-worth that you already possess at your native soul level. Image is *not* everything. A glossy, charming exterior will not protect you from the emptiness of longing for the vital missing element that only your soul can give.

Though this frustration feels like a curse, it is actually a blessing. Eventually you will come to the place where you are ready to consider something more than simply maintaining a polished, well-orchestrated surface image locked in a perpetual acquisitional mode that feeds only your surface 10 percent. You are ready to consider bringing your personality into alignment with your native soul. This alignment is achieved by a willing cooperation that emerges from your quiet times of intuitive listening.

Is Your Desire Image-Driven or Is it Natural?

In order to cooperate with your soul's natural personality alignment process, you must discern whether a desire is image-driven or naturally born from your spiritual center. How do you know the difference? An image-driven desire is *always* motivated by feelings of lack, inadequacy and restlessness, though this may not be readily apparent. You do not overcome fear because you manifest a sum of money or pay off your mortgage or meet a life-partner who lends you their strength and courage and stands with you through whatever challenges life throws your way. You are simply attempting to place your senses-based identity behind a buffering wall while you remain spiritually weak, dependent and unstable.

The question you ask yourself is this: "Am I trying to protect a weakness or am I trying to evolve new strength?"

If you are seeking protection against forces you believe are superior to you or if you are seeking to acquire things or conditions to give you strength, prestige and security, you are attempting to protect some weakness. If you understand your desire as an avenue through which you can express more of your authentic being, if you need to change your conditions because your current ones no longer serve your expanded awareness, then your desire becomes an avenue for evolving new strength.

The Swimming Pool

Consider this example: Bob owns his own plumbing business, works hard and takes good care of his family. They live in a nice home in a quaint neighborhood. But Bob feels something is missing. His neighbor is a surgeon, and Bob is tormented by the surgeon's in-ground swimming pool, often surrounded by laughing children and adults with fancy cocktails. For Bob, the swimming pool is a symbol of success. He's not a doctor, but he works hard. Why shouldn't he have this symbol?

Telling himself he is doing it for his family, he secures a loan and puts in a pool. For weeks he is thrilled watching his family and friends enjoy the pool. He also gleans much satisfaction from showing the world that he is just as successful as the doctor with his fancy degrees. It isn't long, however, before some expensive repairs are needed and Bob has to spend more time at work to cover these and keep up the payment. In addition, he notices his enthusiasm for cleaning and general upkeep is quickly waning. When the pool was new, he did not mind the extra hours required to attend the many details involved in maintenance. Added to the burden of an extra expense is a growing sense of negligence. He knows he needs to spend more time with upkeep, but he just doesn't have the interest he once did. Perhaps the most disturbing revelation is that he now feels no different than he did before he installed the pool.

Bob's youngest daughter, Anne, has a natural swimming ability. She is thrilled when her father installs the pool, for she can practice and become good enough to join the school swim team. For her, inviting in the neighborhood and showing off the pool is an annoying interruption to the time she needs to practice. She makes the swim team and soon discovers an Olympic-sized pool in town. She has little interest in the family pool because it is not designed to enhance her competitive swimming skills. Because she is a natural swimmer, her coach suggests that one day she could compete in the Olympics. This becomes her dream. For Anne, the swimming pool is the medium through which she expresses a natural talent.

In these two scenarios you can see a distinct difference in the relationship with the same item, a swimming pool. The father is using the pool to address a feeling of lack, to satisfy his ego, while the daughter is using it to develop her natural talent and enhance her unique strength.

Spiritual growth is measured, at least in part, by how completely you use your acquisitions as a means of expressing your spiritual authenticity. If you are a natural swimmer and dream of one day competing in the Olympics, you will need a swimming pool to express this potential. If you need a pool to impress others and to feel better about yourself, you will never find one that is good enough or large enough.

Why Did God Do This?

There are other ways that we attempt to protect a weakness while appearing, even to ourselves, to be evolving new strength. A man once came to me asking why God had allowed his marriage to fail. He explained that for eight years after his divorce, he intentionally remained single so he could work on his relationship issues. In his mind he had corrected them, and he was eager to put his hard-earned knowledge, his newly acquired strength, to the test. He remarried, but in a matter of months his new wife had left for another man and the marriage was doomed. Devastated, he held God responsible. "For those eight years I was single," he explained, "I worked hard to get myself right with God. I *deserved* a good marriage and I knew that God was guiding me to make the right choices. Why did God lead me down this path of failure?"

Is it possible for God to lead you down a path of failure? I can think of no circumstance where this would make any sense. If God, the Creative Life Force, is using you as a channel through which more love, life, intelligence and power are expressed, what would be gained by bringing you into circumstances that are stifling and hurtful?

When a person says they have worked hard on themselves and they deserve better, I hear them saying that they've worked hard to build their air-tight, failsafe, image-driven personality and they deserve a reward for all this effort. Attempting to forge your personality into a certain performance for the sake of gaining rewards is like the dog that does backflips for treats. Doing backflips is unnatural to the dog and, were it not for the treat, she would have no interest in performing them. To illustrate this, suppose you are with your dog, treat in hand, enticing her to do a backflip and a squirrel runs through your yard. Your dog instantly abandons the performance *and* the treat in favor of doing what comes natural to her. She takes off after the squirrel, an act that, to her, is itself the treat.

When relationships are approached as the means of getting what you want from life, you can make personality adjustments that will attract your ideal of a mate. But the premise that a relationship can successfully serve you in this way is a gross misunderstanding that creates a burden most relationships simply cannot bear. Like any condition built on spiritual strength, the best relationships are the *effect* of two individuals drawn together because each has either discovered their own natural wholeness or they see this inner discovery as vital to their well being. Such a relationship is far superior to one that depends on the art of doing backflips. There is an unspoken rule that says, *If you have to do backflips to attract the love of your life, you'll have to do double backflips to keep them in your life.*

The image-driven personality that works on itself so God will toss a treat can never be anything more than a high-maintenance mechanism that will likely break down at the most inappropriate time. Simply put, the image-driven personality is incapable of transporting you into the quality of satisfaction you seek. The work you do in this arena may produce a short-term payoff, but it will also effectively block the deeper satisfaction you seek.

I Deserve the Best

Another version of this weakness-protecting attitude is held by those who believe their spiritual heritage alone, though they are out of touch with it, entitles them to the external life they desire. *I am a child of God and I deserve the very best.* Contrived and shallow as it is, the image-driven personality welcomes reinforcement from such platitudes. Unfortunately there is no shortage of effervescent, silver-tongued charlatans who pose as spiritual teachers but peddle this message with the purpose of enriching themselves. They are more than happy to explain why, as a spiritual being, you deserve only the best of the fruit of the land. They are masters at exploiting your frustration and sense of inadequacy. At the end of the day they leave with full pockets, while you leave, inspired perhaps, but still carrying your inadequate personality mechanism.

It is the image-driven personality, struggling to maintain its existence, that claws over the backs of those who get in its way, and there are plenty of people who are willing to do so even under the guise of spiritual development. This spiritually disconnected personality has little regard for the well-being of others and will use them in any way it deems necessary to its survival. It spares no expense, will do harm to those who get in its way, and will even sacrifice its own happiness and well-being to convince others that it has found truth and is successful in its pursuit of peace and prosperity.

The soul-aligned personality does not generate a list of justifications, harbor doubts about whether it deserves something better, or use others to obtain what it knows is already present within its spiritual depths. At your authentic level there is no need to bolster your identity or to make others think you are something more or different. Your native soul is far superior and of much greater value than anything you can accomplish or possess. You do not need to justify having a good relationship, an enriching career, a better home or a more dependable car. The fulfillment of material needs is the natural consequence of expressing in your external world more of your spiritual authenticity.

Hot Air Balloon

A person laboring under the image-driven personality—even one that appears to be grounded in spiritual principle—may fool the world, but they cannot fool the universe. Imagine a man in a hot air balloon trying to gain altitude while dumping his ballast into an onboard trash can. He is afraid to let go of that which has kept him anchored in his shallow perception of reality. He even holds up the empty ballast bags as proof to the world that he has released the weight that keeps him earthbound. All the personality glitz he can muster, however, will not convince the law of gravity. More hot air in his already over-inflated balloon will not do the trick. His inability to gain the internal altitude he seeks demonstrates the wisdom Jesus expressed when he said that nothing remains hidden (beneath even the most shining of personalities) that will not become known (Mt. 10:26). If your balloon basket is skimming the ground, crashing into buildings and catching power lines, you may want to look at where you are dumping your ballast.

When you catch even a glimmer of your native soul, you grasp a much larger, more honest vision of your life's purpose. If a project doesn't work out, there is no reason to assume that God is blocking your success or that you did not deserve to succeed. You see it as a prompt either to go deeper into yourself and discover there is something better, or to further sharpen your skills in ways that enable you to achieve your desire. Apparent failure is often an indication that something better aligned with the integrity of your native soul is unfolding.

Personality Is Not the Culprit

That people commonly use the personality to manipulate, fool, control or otherwise exploit others need not reflect badly on the function of personality itself. Think of your faculty of faith, for example. Though we all possess this faculty, we do not always employ it in a manner that is constructive. Sometimes we pour our faith into the goodness of life, exercising the absolute conviction that all things are working together for our good and for the good of others. Other times we have faith that the world is falling apart. Nothing appears to be working for our good or for the good of anyone else. Though faith can be directed toward the positive or the negative, we neither praise nor condemn the faculty itself for how it is used. This would be like pointing a telescope to the ground and insisting that it is flawed because, looking through the lens, you see no stars. The telescope is not flawed. If you want to see stars then you must point your scope to the heavens.

If you have not already done so, you will reach the point where you understand that all you seek from life is within you. However, turning within does not mean that you begin to think of your personality as deficient, to be eradicated at all costs. Nor is the development of a shining personality key to getting what you want from life. Rather than spend your time and energy developing a personality that will attract the good you seek, know that this interfacing function is self-adjusting. When given the chance, personality will become a beautiful represen-tation of the beauty and power of your native soul. Praise your personality and embrace it as an important outlet of expression for all that you are at your authentic level.

–3–

From Reactionary to Creator

I f you observe yourself closely, you find that much of your life is spent reacting to conditions and people. You feel gloomy because the day is overcast. You are afraid because the economic forecast is dire. You are upset because someone said something unkind, even hurtful. You feel lost because nothing in your life seems to be working. These are examples of a reactionary state of mind. While you may spend much time and energy reacting to people and circumstances, the most effective way of getting what you want from life is to learn to initiate new causes that produce desired effects. Though this is not always the easiest approach, in this chapter we will explore ways of moving from the mindset of a reactionary to the creator of new causes that rise naturally from the authentic level of your being.

Your state of mind is the very essence of your experience, the single most important consideration when you are seeking an improved quality of life. Continually reacting to external circumstances constricts your quality of life. To react is to respond based on the stimulus of a prior action or condition. Your state of mind is tied to previous acts and conditions, as an echo is tied to a sound source. A reaction, therefore, is *responsive* rather

29

than *creative*. Your quality of life is governed by random events and things that are out of your control.

A reaction is often a needed response to conditions. Boarding up windows is a prudent reaction to a hurricane forecast, for example. However, if the bulk of your mental, emotional and physical actions are simply reactions, then you are not initiating the creative new actions that bring your surroundings into conformity with the life you envision.

Let Your Light Shine

When Jesus said, "Let your light shine" (Mt. 5:16), he was telling his followers to do much more than demonstrate love for their fellows by turning on their light of kindness. He was telling them how to change their world from the inside out. Imagine you have a ball of light that you can hold in your hands. Wherever you place this light all darkness dissipates. You peek into a dark closet and you hold your ball of light inside. Now you have a closet filled with light. If you peer into the dark closet and wait for the darkness to disappear before you place your ball of light inside, you will wait forever. You take the action of radiating light as a first cause wherever you go. The world around you reacts by reflecting back the light that shines.

Now imagine that you are that ball of light, but you only let your light shine when conditions are favorable. When conditions are not to your liking, you react by withdrawing your light. Conditions now become the first cause, and your choice of becoming bright or dim is a determination you make based on what happens in the world around you.

Likewise, each day you use your senses of sight and hearing to gather information from surrounding conditions. What you see and hear causes you to decide how you will think, feel and act. The problem with this approach is that it does not take into account the condition of your completed soul that is already fully functioning at the highest level at all times, *regardless* of the state of external conditions. A complete reliance on the senses actually dulls the inner quality of life that is available to you.

What if, like your ball of light, you shone forth with your full luminescence under all conditions? You would stop laboring to sweep away darkness and shadows and focus more on letting your light shine to its full brightness. This is a simple but appropriate example of how to get what you want from life using the spiritual approach. You learn to take a creative rather than reactive attitude toward challenges, to stay on the beam of creativity by bringing your light to bear when things appear to be gloomy. In darkness you grope (react) to find your way. In light your path is clearly illuminated. Light is not caused by first removing darkness. Light itself dispels darkness. Like your imaginary ball of light, your native soul has never known a moment of darkness. *Let your light shine* was the instruction of one of the world's greatest light-bearers and so beautifully acknowledged by that most mystically centered Gospel writer:

> What has come into being in him was life, and the
> life was the light of all people. The light shines in
> the darkness, and the darkness did not overcome it.
> (Jn. 1:3-5)

Removing darkness, in whatever form you perceive it, is not an action you take; it is the natural result of agreeing to let your light shine, of consciously living from your spiritual center. This decision is the first cause you come to know as the healing,

31

balancing influence of the love, life, power and intelligence that is God.

Conditions Are the Past

When you look at the conditions in your life, you are looking into the past, the realm of *effects*. The cause of the effects is not to be found among them. This would be like thinking a sound source is found in the echo it produces. In your approach to creating new conditions, the most important consideration is to treat these desired conditions as effects, not causes. Though you may be curious about the cause of certain effects, it's important to understand that by dwelling on the questions of why and how the conditions have come to pass, you may very well be setting up a new cause that perpetuates the same effect. You may inadvertently create a loop of cause and effect that you will find difficult to escape.

A man born blind was presented to Jesus with the question "Who sinned, this man or his parents?" (Jn. 9:1-7). Jesus did not dwell on how the man's condition of blindness came about. "It was not that this man sinned, or his parents, but that the works of God might be made manifest in him." Jesus focused on and called forth the man's capacity to see.

A fascinating aspect of near-death research involves subjects who are blind. These cases are especially challenging to those steeped in the brain-based model of consciousness. During their out-of-body episodes, blind subjects report in vivid detail events and objects in their material surroundings. Others report experiencing a 360-degree field of vision, suggesting that sight, as we know it, is a restricted version of the native soul's capacity to see. It appears that Jesus was able to call forth this all-seeing capability of the soul, to synchronize the spiritual quality of seeing with its physical counterpart. He could not have done this had he been reacting only to the man's external condition.

I have seen similar transformations, though perhaps on a less dramatic scale, occur frequently in spiritual counseling sessions. I have found that it is not necessary that a spiritual counselor be a trained therapist to facilitate mental and emotional healing. A clear understanding that the person's wholeness is already present, waiting to come forth, is a key to success. My work as a spiritual counselor is to help open the avenue of mind that allows this wholeness to be brought into the realm of effects. While the counselee often feels the need to explain in minute detail every aspect of the negative condition—they are often in full reactionary mode—I listen patiently, gaining the counselee's trust that I understand the problem. At the right moment I will then make as many statements as needed to help the counselee reconnect with his or her wholeness, or at least some aspect of it. The shift that occurs in the counselee brings the effect of wholeness in whatever way is needed, often in a matter of moments.

Turning on Your Light

Whether your need is for healing, prosperity or harmony, making a conscious shift to your wholeness—turning on the light—instantly sets in motion a new cause. This shift in awareness guides your actions and your thinking in creative new ways. Things outside of your immediate awareness also begin to mobilize. God, the Creative Life Force of which your soul is an expression, is omnipresent. There are no gaps in the Divine fabric. When you initiate a new cause, it becomes a center of gravity that draws the elements required for manifestation from all parts of the globe. Shift into this attitude: *My good exists and it is now winging its way toward me!* This, of course, doesn't mean that you sit around and wait for blessings to rain down out of the sky and fall into your hands. Rather, remain focused on your wholeness, the cause that unfolds as the desired condition.

You are designed to initiate causes using your executive faculties of imagination, faith, judgment (your power to choose), will and elimination (your ability to release). You do this most important work in the realm of the unseen, or, as the psalmist called it, the shelter of the Most High.

> You who live in the shelter of the Most High, who abide in the shadow of the Almighty, will say to the Lord, "My refuge and my fortress; my God, in whom I trust." (Ps. 91:1-2)

To initiate a new cause, first use your *imagination* to form an image of the desired condition. You then turn your *faith* on this image. You make choices (*judgment*) that encourage and enhance the manifesting of your vision, releasing (*elimination*) suggestions that would erode your vision and its expression. Faith is the affirmative quality of mind, and elimination is the releasing quality. Faith is opened to spiritual imagery (*intuition*) and elimination is employed to release ideas that are not born of intuition. You employ your *will* to keep the faculties of imagination and faith focused. There is nothing new to learn. You only need to be aware of how you employ these executive faculties in the growing environment of the Creative Life Force.

Spiritual Substance

And what is the nature of this growing environment? Baruch Spinoza, the 17th-century Dutch scientist and philosopher, believed that the myriad of individual forms were but manifestations of an omnipresent, singular energy. Because this energy was thought of as the unseen reality *standing beneath* the visible universe, it acquired the name *substance*, a word that from Spinoza's time to now has been a conceptual staple in metaphysical literature. Charles Fillmore wrote that substance "underlies all manifestation and is the spiritual essence, the living energy out of which everything is made. Through substance all the attributes of Being are expressed" (186-87).

Think of spiritual substance as a freshly tilled garden waiting for all that you envision to grow. In the same way the physical growing environment is comprised of four basic elements—soil, air, sunlight and water—so the spiritual growing environment consists of the four attributes of Being: *life, power, love* and *intelligence*. The native soul, created in the image of God (Gen. 1:26), shares these same attributes.

You discover this spiritual substance in your quiet times of inner reflection when you acknowledge and allow your wholeness to emerge into your field of awareness. You will not think of this inner experience as substance, or break down and analyze its components as I am doing here. But you know the presence of these qualities by their effects on you. Universal love, for example, manifests through you as the *understanding* of what needs to appear and what you need to let go. Love is the great harmonizer and healer, an attracting force that draws to you that which you need while dissolving mental, emotional and material conditions of discord. Love manifests through you as *understanding* of the harmonious reality behind appearances, and it directs you in ways that align your mind, body and affairs with this unseen reality. Divine intelligence expresses through you as *order* in unfolding ideas: *first the stalk, then the head, then the full grain in the head* (Mk. 4:28). Embracing and affirming the presence of Infinite intelligence—*omniscience*—brings this natural order into your mind and your life. You know the attribute of power as *strength* of character and faith in the *omnipotence* of the unseen. And you know the pure energy of life stirring in you as a fountain of *enthusiasm* that nurtures and inspires you.

A spiritually enlightened person consciously draws their being from this inexhaustible source. In addition, they employ their executive faculties in harmony with these attributes, so much so that it is difficult to tell where the Universal ends and the personal begins. *Whoever has seen me has seen the father* (Jn. 14:9). Do not make the mistake of thinking the spiritually enlightened are fundamentally different than you. You are equipped with the identical faculties and fullness of soul of Jesus or anyone else. The difference is found only in the focus of your attention, whether you are drawing your identity from your native soul or from your senses-based experience. Your level of spiritual awareness and understanding dictates how you employ your faculties, and this tendency is responsible for whether your life is internally or externally motivated.

The Parable of the Sower

Jesus created a parable that illustrates a wide range of reasons why, despite the fact that we all rise from the same source, individual lives take on such a wide range of expression.

> Listen! A sower went out to sow. And as he sowed, some seeds fell on the path, and the birds came and ate them up. Other seeds fell on rocky ground, where they did not have much soil, and they sprang up quickly, since they had no depth of soil. But when the sun rose, they were scorched; and since they had no root, they withered away. Other seeds

fell among thorns, and the thorns grew up and choked them. Other seeds fell on good soil and brought forth grain, some a hundredfold, some sixty, some thirty. (Mt. 13:3-8)

This parable is to be understood in the context of the relationship between the Creative Life Force and your consciousness. You will undoubtedly see that you fall in all these places at various times, even within a given day, depending on what draws your attention at the moment.

Think of the sower as the Creative Life Force whose single intention is to express itself through all creation. It is always casting seed, that is, imparting itself as the soul of each person. Jesus explains that the seed represents the "word of the kingdom" (Mt. 13:18-23). The *word*, or *logos*, is the expansive energy that you detect intuitively in your times of quiet meditation. Though everyone receives this word, it is met with varying degrees of understanding, which accounts for the diversity of expression we see within the human family.

The soil type on which the seed falls represents four different levels of awareness. The first three are the most common conditions of consciousness that greatly diminish or prevent a free operating environment for the Creative Life Force within the individual. These are, according to Jesus, the lack of spiritual understanding, distractions caused by troubles of daily living and the pursuit of wealth.

In the first example, the seed lands on a path and is quickly snatched up by birds. This indicates that the individual intuitively senses the inner impulse of the Creative Life Force, is somewhat inspired, but lack of understanding of the source and intention of this inner prompting renders it valueless. The path presents the image of a hardened surface on which nothing can grow. Even if a seed takes root, the frail sprout is in harm's way and will quickly be trampled. The path symbolizes common, well-worn tracks in the human mind, where new ideas are quickly overridden by entrenched ways of thinking. This first type of consciousness represents a person set in their ways, especially when it comes to spiritual matters. Their perception of truth is based on the ideas of others, and they do not believe there is a need to explore any new ideas that may challenge those they hold. They find comfort in catchy clichés. They draw their strength and identity from the groups they join. The practice of closing the eyes and turning to some ambiguous inner source of wisdom is nonsensical, a turning away from "practical" solutions that are to be found somewhere in their surrounding environment.

The second example goes a step further. In this case, the seed actually sprouts and grows. The rocky soil represents a person who entertains some spiritual ideals, but these have no root and quickly wither through the course of a normal day. This person holds beliefs about spiritual concepts, but has not yet transitioned into *knowing*. These beliefs are applied conveniently and in a rather superficial way, so that when things heat up in the withering sun of daily life, they quickly revert to old fears and old methods of overpowering perceived obstacles. At this level, people measure spiritual progress by the state of their material conditions. The primary interest in spiritual teachings is the help they offer in overcoming problems. This category of people attempt to use spiritual principles to protect weaknesses rather than evolve new strengths. Like the first level, the goal is to build an environment that will give them happiness and peace of mind.

According to Jesus, the seed falling among thistles depicts the person who is attracted to spiritual teachings because of their preoccupation with "the cares of the world and the lure of wealth" (Mt. 13:22), a type similar to the second group. Large segments of both Traditional and New Thought adherents seek to apply spiritual principles with the single objective of solving problems by the accumulation of material wealth. At this stage the dominant belief is that wealth produces peace of mind, self-worth, health and—due to the number of books you can purchase and spiritual retreats and seminars you can afford to attend—spiritual enlightenment. Money can indeed bring much good into your life, but it cannot bring into the field of your awareness your native soul and its relationship to the Infinite.

In varying degrees, these three levels of consciousness are all motivated by the belief that possessions—mental, emotional and material—hold the key to fulfillment. Obtaining more possessions, therefore, is the real motive behind gaining spiritual understanding. The purest and highest motive for acquiring spiritual understanding, however, is for the understanding itself. Of course your understanding of the spiritual dimension must include the all-important connection between the condition of your consciousness and the way it translates as your material conditions.

By including the fourth illustration—seed falling in good soil, sprouting and producing at varying levels—Jesus indicates that spiritual understanding indeed has a relevant and positive bearing on your external life. The point he seems to be making with the different yields is that your material demonstration varies according to your grasp of how the unseen translates into the visible. Even a 30-fold yield, the lowest in his illustration, is superior to the results produced in the previous three examples.

You are perpetually receiving the expansive impulse of the Creative Life Force and it is through regular periods of meditation that you open your intuitive portal and come to know it firsthand. The regular practice of meditation builds a consciousness that recognizes God as your permanent source. This is important because the distinguishing aspect of your life comes down to the unique way in which you employ your executive faculties. You are imprinting upon the Creative Life Force the pattern that ultimately manifests as your external conditions. Your beliefs determine the types of choices you make and your choices guide your actions. If you are doing this blindly and haphazardly, you will get poor results. A conscious alignment with your spiritual Source brings your faculties into harmony and attracts a material environment equivalent to the abundance you experience in your silent depths.

The importance of the parable is that it illustrates that your external conditions will improve with your understanding of spiritual law. "Seek first his kingdom and his righteousness, and all these things will be given to you as well" (Mt. 6:33). Jesus does not undermine the value of a healthy body and a prosperous material life. Rather he treats these as the *effects* that follow the deeper understanding of your relation to the Infinite. If you approach your spiritual studies simply for the purpose of converting the Creative Life Force into cash, health or advantageous material conditions, you will fail to discover your permanent source and miss completely the surest, most dependable and accessible resource for getting what you want from life.

Reconnect With Your Essence

When your beliefs are grounded strictly in material appearances, your thoughts and actions are influenced by the problem as it appears to you. This makes it nearly impossible to resolve the problem from your fixed point of view. The time comes when you catch yourself in this endless reactive cycle and begin instead to let go of the appearance and reconnect to the deeper, changeless essence of your being, a process that allows the appearance to break up, like a debris jam in a river, and flow with the current.

H. Emilie Cady shares a wonderful example of this dynamic in the introduction to her book, *How I Used Truth*. She tells the story of how her father had been kept in exile for five years, "put there by the wicked machinations of another man. No process of law that I had invoked, no human help, not even the prayers that I had offered had seemed to avail for his deliverance" (135). One day, while occupied with other things, her heart cried out, "O God, stretch forth Thy hand and deliver!" The answer came immediately. "Your hand is my hand; stretch it forth spiritually and give whatsoever you will to whomsoever you will, and I will establish it." In that instant she realized that she was the channel through which the Infinite would work. "From that moment," she writes, "without any further external help or striving, the way of his [her father's] release was opened ahead of us more rapidly almost than we could step into it. Within a few days my dear father came home a free man, justified, exonerated, both publicly and privately, beyond anything we could have asked or thought" (136).

While working hard at solving the problem, Dr. Cady could not see a way through. Judging by appearances, she found that legal action, advice from others and even prayer failed to produce the answer she needed. Once she stopped reacting to the situation by turning her attention elsewhere, she inadvertently assumed a more receptive mode and the solution came.

Gaining New Perspective

Imagine losing your way in a forest. You are convinced that you are traveling in the right direction. Time passes and still nothing looks familiar. You are beginning to have doubts. You decide to climb to a rock outcropping and look for landmarks that will help you find your way. There you discover that you were actually moving in the wrong direction.

Climbing the outcropping may seem like it has nothing to do with attaining your desired destination, but the view it affords proves to be invaluable. The vision you gain by releasing your perception and moving inwardly to higher ground becomes the new cause ensuring that either more suitable conditions are stimulated or you experience new insight into the conditions that surround you now and utilize them in ways that are beneficial and productive.

If you discover that you need to change direction, you have to let go of the direction you have been going. You may associate *letting go* with inaction or ignoring a problem, but letting go means that you release yourself from a type of thinking that obligates you to see the problem from an unworkable level. The spiritual approach does not ignore the problem. Rather, it allows you to approach it from a higher point of view. Remember that spiritual power is not a force that overcomes negativity but rather the energy that raises your vision above the level of the perceived problem. When this shift in perception occurs, the way through the appearance, as in H. Emilie Cady's case, is seen, and often very quickly. Getting inspirational leads from others is sometimes an important and welcome step, but learning to draw from your own inner well is the only way you will align your consciousness with your native soul. This alignment is the goal of everything associated with spiritual practice. When properly understood, meditation accomplishes this synchronization of consciousness and soul, the good soil and the sower.

The Flexible Will

You may equate the exercise of your *will* with a hardened choice to move in a particular direction with unbending force, often with unpleasant consequences. *I'm supposed to think positively, so I will force myself to do so.* This reflects the attitude of one who refuses to see all options. In contrast, the attitude of *I am willing to take an expanded and more positive approach to this situation* reflects the kind of flexibility needed to move from a rigid stand that may be headed in the wrong direction to one that is open to all possibility. The first is similar to insisting on completing an electrical circuit with a piece of wood; the second is completing the circuit with a strand of copper wire. Both are an exercise of the will, but the second attitude is most conducive to the fluid movement of spiritual energy.

You may turn to God for specific answers you hope will change things. When you understand God as the Creative Life Force, you see that God empowers you with life, love, intelligence and power. "Your hand is my hand," as H. Emilie Cady realized. "Stretch it forth spiritually." You are the one making the decisions on how you will bring these universal energies into your affairs. When you are in a reactionary mode, you empower appearances in ways that often strengthen their condition. When you move into the creative mode that recognizes God as your unfailing Source and support, your life will begin to yield the type of conditions that are satisfying.

The irony is that you have used your most powerful executive faculty, your *imagination*, to envision yourself as lacking the very fulfillment that you seek. In the next chapter, we will examine this faculty in depth and see the dual role it must play in allowing the fullness of your native soul to shine forth in all of its fullness of strength and beauty.

4

Your Creative Imagination

The aim of meditation is to gain understanding of your spiritual source through direct exposure to your core being. Because God as the Creative Life Force is not physically observable, you must learn to experience God through nonphysical means. "God is spirit, and those who worship him must worship in spirit and truth" (Jn. 4:24). Jesus rightfully compared the Divine Presence to the wind that blows where it chooses. You hear the sound of it, but you do not know where it comes from or where it goes (Jn. 3:8). The Creative Life Force, though invisible to the eye, is just as real as the wind that sighs through the leaves or pushes the sailboat across the sea.

When you think of the faculty that enables you to perceive God, you may, like most, think of intuition rather than imagination. After all, intuitive knowledge is defined as that which is directly perceived without the use of the senses. The imagination, on the other hand, is generally depicted as the creative, image-generating and objectifying faculty of mind. The faculty of imagination actually performs *both* functions. In its intuitive function, it is the inlet, a direct pipeline to the pure essence of Being. In its image-generating function, it converts the pure energy of Spirit into the vision that becomes the basis for the life you project in the material world. Charles Fillmore explained it this way:

> In the communication of God with man, the imagining power of the mind plays an important part. It *receives* divine ideas and *reflects* their character to the consciousness. (104)

The receiving aspect of your imagination is your *intuitive* ability, a portal capable of opening directly to the universal forces of the spiritual dimension. All living things possess this intuitive aspect of the imagination. In Nature we see the essential characteristics of Being—*life, power, intelligence* and *love*—manifested as a balanced, perfectly integrated symphony orchestra with every section, while playing different parts, complementing the whole. What is absent or at least greatly restricted in the natural world is the visioning aspect of the imagination. Possession of this ability to visualize sets the human species apart from all others. This visioning aspect, which is an important part of the *intellect*, allows us to develop a personal rather than a generic vision of ourselves and our life, an ability that has placed our species in a very unique position in Nature.

We have, to a great extent, shut down the portal of intuition and drawn our guiding information from the wide open gates of sensory input. The imagination has fallen under the direction of the senses-driven intellect that insists the facts presented by external appearances represent ultimate reality. We are elated or traumatized according to this steady input that has little in common with the unchanging reality that can only be perceived intuitively. It is as if we are riding in a glass bottom boat gliding over warm waters rich in aquatic wonders, but a carpet covers the glass. We are essentially cut off from the stabilizing serenity and beauty that exists beneath our ever-changing surface life.

The Digital Camera

To understand how these intuitive and reflective aspects of the imagination are intended to work as a single creative function, we can turn to the digital camera for an illustration. The beauty of digital cameras, particularly the point-and-shoot models, is their simplicity. Point the camera at your subject—a person, a landscape or a flower—and press the shutter button. The camera, automatically sensing light conditions, presents you with an impressive replica of the image you see in the camera's viewfinder.

Simplicity at the user end does not mean there is anything simple about the camera's process. The instant you snap the shutter, a series of small miracles of science occurs. Light reflected from your subject passes through the lens to the camera's image sensor. The light is first converted into an electrical signal that is then translated into digital information through the camera's processor. Once the image becomes digitized, you can email it around the world, project it onto a screen or print it to paper as a photograph. The camera plays the dual role of receiving the *universal* energy of light and combining it with a *personal* choice of imagery.

Most digital cameras are equipped with a small liquid crystal display (LCD) that allows you to see (compose) your image before you actually snap the shot. Think of this viewfinder as equivalent to the mental screen of your imagination. To capture the image that you see on your viewfinder, you introduce a burst of light onto the image sensor by snapping the shutter button. With this simple act, you combine the *universal* energy of light with your *personal* choice of imagery. Your camera's computer then translates this combination of energy and imagery into the digital information that you share with the world as a photograph. Here you have a perfect illustration of how universal energy (light) is combined with personal choice (the image in your viewfinder) to create a specific condition (your photograph).

Now think of the intuitive side of your imagination as your camera's shutter. Through the intuition flows the universal energy of life, power, love and intelligence. This energy combines with the picture-forming aspect of your imagination (your mental viewfinder) to produce a state of consciousness (equivalent to the digital platform) that serves as the basis for your material conditions. These states of consciousness comprise the unique photo gallery that you call your life. It is within the imagination that the personal and the universal are brought together to form the unique basis of your external life conditions. Rather than generating digital information that a computer understands, you generate states of consciousness that serve as the basis for your unique material conditions.

For many, this blending of the universal and the personal is a random and unconscious process, like snapping photos all day long at nothing in particular. At the end of the day they review these photos and discover they have no meaning. They are not getting what they want from life because of their haphazard employment of their imagination.

To further the analogy, consider the difference in image quality taken in artificial and natural light. The average flash photo is often harsh and washed out while natural sunlight, at the right time of the day, is soft and warm. Professional photographers love those 20-minute windows of light that occur just after dawn and again just before dusk. In this natural light even an amateur photographer can obtain impressive results. Fact-based, intellectual knowledge is harsh and washed out in comparison to the warmth of light that rises through the intuitive portal of the soul.

Uniquely Human

The evolution of the visioning, personalizing aspect of the imagination has placed the human family in a unique position in nature. Unlike the plant and animal kingdoms, there appears to be no natural limits to the effects we can produce through the creative application of our imagination. Its usage is a subject that warrants careful consideration.

Thomas Troward, English author and lecturer who had a significant impact on the early development of mental science, made the profoundly simple observation that the human being is the only creature capable of producing ideas that do not occur spontaneously in nature (4). Place a lump of iron in water, he noted, and the iron sinks, an effect governed by natural law, or, as Troward called it, *generic law*. Fabricate that same iron into the hull of a ship and the iron will float. The iron hull, like countless other examples we could name, is a product of the human imagination, a unique combination of universal energy and personal imagery.

Though plants and animals display varying levels of intelligence and personality, they are restricted by a natural barrier in their creative ability. Troward attributed this to the animal's inability to express anything more than generic law. Think of generic law as the expression of the Creative Life Force without any elaboration of human imagination. The lump of iron, governed by generic law, sinks in water. Introduce the influence of human imagination and the iron is able to float. Nature as a whole is an example of generic law in expression.

People often ask whether or not animals have souls. Using Troward's model, the answer would be yes, but it is a *generic soul*, an archetypal set of parameters that limit the expression of intelligence and, therefore, the creative capacity of a given species. The key limiting element in the generic soul of all living things (though it is present in nearly all species in limited degrees) is the visualizing aspect of imagination.

For survival and reproductive purposes, animals depend on a preprogrammed set of responses we know as *instinct*. Yes, there are cases where chimpanzees fish termites from their mounds with sticks and certain birds break open ostrich eggs by bombarding them with stones. These, however, can hardly be thought of as anything more than examples of intelligence still bridled by a rudimentary imagination.

If you own a dog, you know it as an intelligent animal with a unique personality. Personable and intelligent as your dog may be, however, you can safely assume it will never be credited with a medical breakthrough, never send other dogs to Mars or develop a faster, more efficient Internet. The intelligence level of the brightest dog on the planet (yours no doubt) is primitive in comparison to that of even a below-average human. This may seem unflattering to those who insist on elevating their dogs to near-human status, but experts in canine behavior know the key to successful interaction between dog and human is to get the human to start thinking like a dog. The dog, they know, can never think like the human. The dog simply does not possess the imaginative capacity of the human.

The Generic Cap

This concept of a generic soul can explain why, in contrast to the sometimes chaotic experience we see at the human level, the natural world exists in such balance and harmony. Nature has no choice. It is a material representation of the Creative Life Force capped by a generic imagination. Plants and animals get creative when it comes to snaring food, reproducing and even shelter-building. But if you observe a herd of 100,000 wildebeests, you see that each one leads a very similar life. Their choices of food, habitat and behavior are nearly identical throughout the herd. Roll back the clock a million years and you are likely to see the same basic wildebeest behavior.

By contrast, visit any town of 100,000 people and you will see countless economic, cultural, political, religious and lifestyle distinctions. The evolution of the faculty of imagination, the ability to combine universal energy with personal imagery, has lifted the human species beyond the creative restrictions of basic instinct. The Lascaux cave paintings in southern France, dating back 16,000 years, clearly illustrate the emerging artistic tendency in our race. In Utah, I visited a site containing ancient rock art of a scene depicting a shaman assisting in hunting success. This scene contains all the elements you find in a modern *vision board* and illustrates that people have long understood the role and importance of the visualizing aspect of imagination.

Our modern cultures have invented an entirely new world full of houses with beautifully landscaped yards, glistening high-rise cities, bustling shopping malls, countless educational opportunities, grocery stores with foods from around the world, sophisticated transportation systems, instant global communications, trade and manufacturing that has literally altered the landscape of the planet. Roll back the clock a million years and, unlike the wildebeest, you will see a humanity that scarcely resembles the modern version.

Like animals, we, too, have a generic soul, but our turbocharged faculty of imagination has allowed us to take giant creative leaps far beyond the circumscribed boundaries that inhibit the creativity of other species. Your dog loves you unconditionally, and you would like to think it is because he lives on a higher level of awareness. In truth, he is forgiving because he simply cannot read anything into the fact that you forgot to feed him yesterday. He takes the food you give him today as if you are the most wonderful, thoughtful provider on earth. He cannot curse you for the discomfort you may have caused, nor can he attribute your forgetfulness to one of your unresolved childhood issues. He wags his tail in loving gratitude that he is finally eating again. He is hardwired to love and trust you, his pack leader, and he cannot engage in behavior that is inconsistent with his generic soul.

It may seem that animal vitality and the ability to be fully present can be attributed to the animal having attained a superior level of awareness. This ability, however, is better explained as the animal's inability to conceive of the abstract concepts of future or past. Nearly all their faculties are programmed to address their present needs. They function from a model of success that is limited to the threefold aim of filling their bellies, finding shelter and reproducing offspring. Animals may be content with this basic agenda, but the spiritually awakening human, who has no apparent inventive restrictions, is not.

From Simplicity to Complexity

Your life feels incomplete when you project from the perception that you are separated from your spiritual foundation, your native soul. Your soul is a concentration of life, love, power and intelligence inherent in the Creative Life Force. Your faculty of imagination allows you to personalize these elements to produce all the various aspects of your life. As I pointed out with the camera illustration, you do this by first establishing centers of thought that become states of consciousness, and these, in turn, serve as centers from which specific things and conditions evolve.

It may seem an oversimplification to say that our life, as it is expressed, is derived from varying combinations of four basic elements. Consider that, from a computer standpoint, each letter in our English alphabet is created from binary code. Letters are a unique combination of two digits, 0 and 1, put together in a string of eight. For example, you see the capital letter "L," but the computer sees 01001100. You see the word *love* (in lower case), and the computer sees 11011000100111101110110011001100101. When you consider the range of ideas that are communicated by varying combinations of these two digits, you see how complexity can grow out of simplicity. Depending on the human imagination to which they are subjected, two digits can convey everything from the obscene to the divine. Complicating the code by adding a third or fourth digit would not change the nature of ideas individuals wish to convey. Two digits are sufficient to convey any idea that can be put into language.

From this perspective, you can see that asking God to give you something that will make you feel more complete is asking the impossible. All of God's attributes, like a spiritual binary code, are present and are being perpetually imparted to every person and to every living thing. Your feeling of incompleteness is based on the illusion that your soul is undeveloped, separate from its source or lacking crucial information. As you awaken to your unity with the Infinite, you begin to understand that your very existence is an activity of the Creative Life Force, and that your desire for a fuller, more expanded life is nothing less than the inner stirring of your completed soul. When you start with the awareness that all creative forces are concentrated within you and are therefore available for your use, you begin to apprehend and project from your wholeness into your external affairs and you begin to get what you want from life.

The Example of Three Artists

Imagine three artists being given identical palettes containing six colors of paint each—violet, blue, green, yellow, orange and red. At this stage these unused colors are in a universal state or, using Troward's term, *generic* state. The paints, equally available to all three artists, have not been combined into any specific image. The artists begin mixing their colors and applying brush strokes according to their individual preferences and understanding. Though they have drawn from the same universal set of colors, the final work produced by each is as unique in color combination and form as the personalities of the artists themselves. They transform these colors into something truly their own. Their results are profoundly different.

In the same way the full range of colors is available to each artist, so the full range of divine attributes is available to every person. How you combine and express these attributes is completely up to you. You might be tempted to think that getting what you want from life requires you to ask God, "What picture do you want me to paint?" God can no more answer this question than can the palette of paint tell the artist what kind of picture she should create. God supplies you with the palette and the faculty of imagination and says, "The picture you paint is up to you." The combination of your understanding, your vision and your skill as a painter determines the nature and quality of your results.

You, like the painter, are accessing and utilizing divine qualities in the way that is translating into your material life. You are drawing from the universal palette of color, and you are painting your life based on the beliefs you hold. If you are unhappy with what you see on your canvas, it is useless to ask God to guide you to a different palette of colors or to expect God to fix your painting. There is no other palette and the Creative Life Force cannot magically change your circumstances. Outside of you, this divine force can only act generically. It cannot act creatively, at least not in the specific ways you need or desire. The specifics of how it is expressed in your life depend on how you employ your executive faculties, specifically the visioning aspect of your imagination.

You Are Directing God

In a very real sense, and this may come as a surprise, your life is the result of the directives you are giving to God. To return again to our earlier example, you are composing images in your viewfinder and bringing in universal energy to create the photo album that is your life. Be assured, you have a very willing partner who has given you unconditional support in bringing forth the exact world you envision. God does not say, "Are you sure you want this or that picture?" Without you the

Creative Life Force performs generically, producing beautiful and endless combinations of life, love, intelligence and power, but with no ability to deviate from the inherent constraints of each expression's generic parameters. With you in the picture, the same creative process is at work but without constraints. You add to the creative process the expanded influence of your executive faculties that you employ in accordance to your understanding. The life you know and live is the result.

Though there are times when it may appear to do so, the Creative Life Force does not impart specific solutions to your needs, at least not in the way you may think. It imparts its full range of characteristics always. Scripture tells us that "God is light" (1 Jn. 1:5), and indeed light provides yet another excellent way to illustrate this point. Place a prism anywhere there is a beam of sunlight and you will, without exception, see the entire visible spectrum of color. If you said to a beam of sunlight, "I need more blue," it would not give you blue only; it would give you the entire spectrum. It cannot do otherwise. You can use a filter that allows only the blue frequency to pass, but the full spectrum is still always present.

In the same way the full spectrum of colors is present in the beam of sunlight, so *all* the qualities that constitute the Creative Life Force are present everyplace equally at once. Most important, they are always present in and as you. So how do you find solutions to specific problems? Consider how a single sunset can inspire countless expressions of music, poetry, photography, paintings and other forms of artistic expression. Peering directly into the Creative Life Force charges the visual aspect of your imagination with endless ideas that can be combined into an infinite range of states of consciousness that are as unique as you, the individual projecting them. Solutions to specific problems unfold with this influx of pure inspiration. New life sparks enthusiasm. Divine power stirs unbounded strength to move forward. Intelligence kindles the flame of wisdom, and love deepens and opens the understanding. As the author of Job so eloquently put it:

> It is the spirit in a mortal, the breath of the Almighty,
> that makes for understanding. (Job 32:8)

As your mind expands with new inspiration, you compose in the *viewfinder* of your imagination ideas and actions that are natural to you and address constructively and precisely the issues involved with your particular situation. Your native soul is as unique as your fingerprint. Given the chance, it will present you with an equally unique opportunity to transform your seeming problem into a creatively exciting endeavor.

5

The Manifestation Process

In approaching the subject of the manifestation process, there are a couple of things that should be understood. The most obvious is a fact we have already considered: You are now fully engaged in the manifestation process. You are a spiritual being expressing through a physical body surrounded by a set of circumstances that are unique to you. You yourself are an example of the invisible becoming visible. You neither start nor stop this process, but you do influence results. The idea is to understand *how* you influence results and make deliberate choices to influence them in ways that better contribute to the quality of life you desire. Later in this chapter, we will look at five steps of the manifestation process. As you will see, aside from refocusing the manner in which you employ your executive faculties, you have nothing new to learn. Before we get to the five-step process, I want to share a few ideas that I think will be helpful.

The Role of Will

The faculty of *will* plays a vital role in the manifestation process, but in a way that may be quite different than you think. Many see the exercise of will as coercing people and conditions to conform to their wishes. The will is best understood as the means of keeping our executive faculties in focus and on track. Like the rudder on a ship, the will keeps you on course even in the shifting winds of change.

When you set out in any new direction, things typically start smooth and as expected. Optimism comes easy, and you feel strong and alive with creativity. Then something changes unexpectedly, and though you manage to correct it, self-doubt creeps in. Time passes and your anticipated success seems no closer. You become plagued with images of failure and your faith in yourself and your desire begins to wane. It is here that your faculty of will comes into play.

You will yourself to let go of these visions (elimination), to turn within and to reopen to God the intuitive portal of your imagination. Your faith, which was beginning to veer toward self-doubt and fear of impending failure, is brought back into focus by your firm and steady act of will. Your appearance-based judgment, which had you ready to abandon your desire, is brought back to choice-making that supports your desire. Rather than manipulate external conditions or people, your will is employed to influence your own executive faculties.

The importance of this distinction cannot be overstated. Forcing our will on people and circumstances with the sole aim of getting what we want is the kind of activity that has given willpower a bad name. People involved in sales often exert this type of willpower over their customers. They respond to the customer's every objection with the single goal of changing the customer's mind and making a sale. The best sales people are those who place high value on the customer's actual needs and interests. They use their will to stay focused on what they can give rather than on what they can get from the customer.

Keeping one's own faculties in line with what is highest and best for all is a quiet activity that intrudes on no one.

While many of your life situations illustrate the manifestation process in action and can teach you much, you also live in a virtual classroom conducted by the most profound teachers available: simple things that are so common you may fail to see their relevance to your own experience.

The Wisdom of a Bean

On several different occasions through my childhood, I remember planting common navy beans in coffee cans and watching in wonder as they grew to maturity. Those many years ago, I made no connection between the bean's transformation and the manifestation process as it applied to my life. Having become more spiritually perceptive, I now see that all the principles illustrated in the growing bean are perpetually at work in each of us. So much so that I once gave a series of talks based on the premise that everything you need to know about prosperity and the manifestation process you can learn from a lowly bean.

When you hold a bean in your hand, for example, you are holding a tiny package of potential that has the ability to grow into a full plant. The vision you hold for your life, like the bean, contains the potential for the full expression of your desired condition. For this transformation to occur, both the bean and your vision are subjected to a transformational process in which things unseen are made visible. In the case of the bean, it must die to its bean identity; otherwise it will remain a bean. You can store it in a jar forever and it will remain dormant. To start this transforming process, you plant your bean in soil. The same principles hold true of your vision. You can carry it within your mind forever and it will remain little more than a fanciful possibility that you visit only in your dreams. You plant your vision in the spiritual substance of life, love, power and intelligence. Both the bean and your vision require care after planting. Just as you water the bean, you pour your faith into your vision. You place your bean in sunlight, which is the equivalent to placing your vision into the universal intelligence and energy that charges it with life and transforms it from the invisible to the visible. Later, we'll see all these aspects incorporated in the five-step manifestation process.

Thinking of your life as it is, you can see all its various aspects represent a composite of seed you have planted. Changing any aspect requires the dual process of letting go of something old and taking on something new, similar to removing the remnants of an old crop and replanting another. There is a difference, however. You can pull and toss an old bean plant without giving it any thought. Letting go of life conditions that no longer work for you is different in that you have placed sentimental values on the old conditions. If these are not handled properly, they will cause interference with bringing forth the new. In this case, the process is not unlike moving a household to a new location. Moving does not mean that you put the brakes on the manifestation process in one area and start it anew in another. The manifestation process never ceases. You, however, redirect your focus. With your mind open to a new destination, you go through your entire household and decide what you will keep and what you will let go. Sorting through your accumulation of things demonstrates the complexity of your consciousness. Every item tells stories of people, places, sounds, smells and states of mind, some of which you remember and some you had forgotten.

In the household of your mind you carry many mental objects that generate streams of thought and emotion, some pleasant, some not. Taken as a whole, these mental objects make up your consciousness and serve as a major influence on the manifestation process. As we've already discussed, the nucleus of your consciousness is your self-image. You hold certain types of thought objects because of who you believe you are.

The reason meditation can have a major impact on your external life is that, when properly engaged, it transforms the very heart around which your entire consciousness revolves.

When you begin to experience your spiritual wholeness, you let go of many things you once believed you needed. You are, in a sense, like the paralytic man that lay on a mat by the pool of Beth-zatha for 38 years (Jn. 5:2-9). Jesus told him to pick up the mat and walk. After walking for a time, still clinging to his mat, he would realize that he no longer needed it as a constant accessory for his daily experience. You, too, will be confronted with many such decisions. The choices you make in letting go of the old and taking up the new will have a significant impact on how quickly you bring forth your desired vision.

The Manifestation Process

I have discovered, buried in the writings of Thomas Troward, five steps for bringing all your faculties to bear on a specified goal. The advantage of using such steps is that they provide you with a distinct course of action enabling you to become conscious of how you employ your executive faculties of faith, imagination, judgment, will and elimination. For this or any goal-setting method, however, it is imperative to keep in mind that the most influential goal is that of spiritual self-discovery. Goals that are designed to compensate for feelings of lack and inadequacy will not produce the results you seek. For an in-depth discussion on this topic, I recommend reading the revised edition of my book *A Practical Guide to Prosperous Living*, and particularly Chapter 9, "The Goal of Your Goal."

The five steps put forth by Troward and modified by me are as follows:

Step 1: Form a clear picture of your desire with the understanding that, by so doing, you create a prototype that is impressed upon the Creative Life Force.

Step 2: Understand that you are working with spiritual law. With calm expectation of a corresponding result, know that all necessary conditions are coming about in proper order.

Step 3: Enter your daily routine with the assurance that conditions are either present already or will soon present themselves. If you do not see evidence at once, know that the spiritual prototype (your desire) is already in existence.

Step 4: Wait until some circumstance pointing in the desired direction begins to show itself. It may be small, but it is the type and not the magnitude of the circumstance that is important. This is the first sprouting of the seed.

Step 5: Do whatever the circumstance seems to require. This action leads to the further unfolding of other circumstances in the same direction. By addressing each one as it appears, you move step by step toward the accomplishment of your desire.

As you can see, these steps are both natural and familiar activities that you engage in all the time. Let's take a closer look at each one.

Step 1: *Form a clear picture of your desire with the understanding that, by so doing, you create a prototype that is impressed upon the Creative Life Force.*

This first step requires that you create a clear picture of your desire and that you treat this picture as a *real* thing, a prototype of the material condition you wish to establish. A prototype, as you know, is the original form of something. It has the essential features and is the model for the material form to follow.

As I've already indicated, the self-image you carry is actually the prototype for the life you are now experiencing. This understanding should prompt you to weigh each desire against the question of whether you are attempting to protect a weakness or bring forth more of your native soul. It is important to know that you cannot treat the manifestation process as an isolated mechanism that you turn on or off at will or that you can employ with laser-like precision to just one facet of your life. This process is translating *all* of what you think of yourself at *all* times and under *all* circumstances. Being clear about your motives brings you in line with the complete life landscape you desire to express.

Ideas are real things, the foundational blueprints of the manifestations that follow. All invention begins with an idea that is later converted into a material object. As Charles Fillmore observed:

Everything is first an idea in mind, and this law holds good, not only in the creations of God, but in the forms made by man as well. The table upon which you write was first an idea in the mind of the maker. (*The Revealing Word* 101)

How do you create a clear picture of a desire involving aspects you cannot possibly know? You start at your feeling level. What feelings do you hope to accomplish with the attainment of this desire? Write your responses to this question. At this early stage, do not be concerned about the form or length of your writing. Take more time to revise and condense your ideas into sentences that take the form of denials (statements of release) and affirmations (statements designed to establish an idea in your consciousness).

Once you have a clear vision of your desire, you must make the deliberate choice to use your executive faculties to carry it out. As I pointed out earlier, your *faith* is the expectation that your desire is a real thing that is now coming forth. Your *imagination* is the inlet for the universal life, love, power and intelligence of the Creative Life Force. Keep yourself open to the Universal through meditation. Your imagination is also the projecting mechanism that allows you to personalize this picture you initiate as a creative *cause*. You exercise *judgment* in choosing the types of thoughts and emotions you hold, carefully choosing those that support your imagery as well as the truth you experience in your spiritually receptive times. Through your faculty of *elimination* you release doubt and concern about how your desire will come into being. This releasing of doubt enables you to go about the business of your daily life knowing that you are cooperating with the Creative Life Force in bringing forth your desire. Finally you employ your *will*, not as a forceful means of manipulating people and circumstances into giving you what you want, but as the directive power that keeps all your faculties working in concert toward your desired end.

In the same way that you, a spiritual being, are complete, so your desire, in its prototypical form, is complete once you accept it as yours. This is similar to seeing the complete image in your camera's viewfinder before you snap a shot. The light that enlivens your composition is always present and you are not responsible for creating the light. Likewise, you do not start the manifestation process just because you create a complete image of your desire. The manifestation process is in perpetual operation. If your image is incomplete and unclear, this will be reflected in your manifestation. The act of forming a distinct vision of your desire immediately begins to influence the manifestation process. You cannot start or stop it; you only influence what it produces in your life.

If you are visually oriented, you may find it helpful to develop a vision board, a poster board of images and statements that assist you in working out your vision and holding a clear picture. If you are computer-oriented, you will find a powerful visualizing tool in Microsoft's PowerPoint program or its free Open Office counterpart. With these programs, you can develop a slide show that incorporates the five steps, using your own statements and images that best represent the vision you wish to bring forth. The Internet is a great source of images you can download.

The ancients apparently saw the value in this type of exercise. Throughout the American West there are countless examples of images chipped or painted on the stone walls of cliffs depicting hunting success, bountiful harvests, spiritual protection and sustained fertility. One notable panel in the Nine Mile Canyon area of Utah, known as the Hunting Scene, depicts a herd of desert bighorn sheep all moving toward hunters poised with bow and arrow. Among the sheep is a horned figure some believe represents a shaman, a spiritual component working on behalf of the hunters. The scene clearly illustrates the ancients' understanding of the law of attraction. As I sat before this large panel, I could imagine hunters gathering before a hunt and taking in this scene as a powerful way of affirming success.

Step 2: *Understand that you are working with spiritual law. With calm expectation of a corresponding result, know that all necessary conditions are coming about in proper order.*

Drawing again from the realm of agriculture, Jesus gives some important clues as to how to think of the manifestation process.

> The kingdom of God is as if someone would scatter seed on the ground, and would sleep and rise night and day, and the seed would sprout and grow, he does not know how. The earth produces of itself, first the stalk, then the head, then the full grain in the head. (Mk. 4:26-28)

By developing and holding your specific vision, you are working with spiritual law and your manifestation comes about through an orderly process. This understanding not only inspires the strength to continue holding your vision, it also inspires you to do it with enthusiasm. This is a *calm* but passionate interest in bringing forth your vision. Emerson acknowledged: "Nothing great was ever achieved without enthusiasm." Enthusiasm is the energy of life, but enthusiasm not tempered with calm understanding becomes a drain. As Psalm 69:9 puts it, "It is zeal for your house that has consumed me." Exciting times can take as much of a toll on your peace of mind as difficult times. Losing sleep when you are excited is as stressful as losing sleep when you are worried. Calm expectation, *faith*, suggests a state of mind where you lose no sleep at all.

Step 3: *Enter your daily routine with the assurance that conditions are either present already or will soon present themselves. If*

you do not see evidence at once, know that the spiritual pro-
totype (your desire) is already in existence.

This step is simply a reminder to remain steadfast with your vision throughout the activities of your day. If you continually move your camera from this scene to that, never locking in on a shot, you will have much activity in your viewfinder but you will get no pictures. When you commit to holding an image of your desire, do not allow distractions, indifference, doubt or fear to marginalize your vision. It is often easier to chase after every little thing that captures your attention than to stay steadily focused on the things you value. Throughout the day, your vision will pale and feel like a dream that is small and distant, seemingly impossible to achieve. These daily activities demand your attention and wrench you away from your vision. It is in the face of these mundane distractions that require your greatest strength and assertion of will to keep your faculties focused.

I'm not suggesting that you plant your bean seed and then sit next to it, holding the picture on the package in your hand, praying day in and day out with all the intensity you can muster, willing the seed to sprout and begin to look like the picture. What an unnecessary labor and use of your executive faculties this would be! And yet this is a reasonable description of how many approach the manifestation process.

Nor do you plant your bean and go about your daily routine as if all your happiness and freedom depended on its growth. You do not expect the bean to grow and pluck you from circumstances you do not want. You do not think it will take you away from a tyrant of a boss who discounts your accomplishments and accentuates your mistakes. Nor do you expect your bean to produce enough money to solve all of your problems of the present and future. If you heap this kind of energy on your seed, it will disappoint you because it will do none of these things. There is even the possibility that your forced willfulness and misdirected expectations may stunt the growth of your plant.

Rather, you plant your seed and go about your business with the calm assurance that something greater than you is taking over. You attend your seed with daily watering and loving care. You may think fondly of this tiny miracle and watch with anticipation for signs of the first sprout appearing above the soil's surface. If you see no sprout, you still know your seed is planted, and that it is only a matter of time before you start seeing results.

Approach your desire in exactly the same way. Your prototype, like the bean, exists as a very real thing in the fertile growing environment, the spiritual substance of life, power, love and intelligence, the Creative Life Force that knows how to bring forth the desires of your heart. If you go about your daily routine looking for evidence that your vision is sprouting and you see no evidence, you begin to doubt that anything is happening. You question your right to have the life you desire. You believe you are not spiritually mature enough to employ this transforming type of approach. You resign to continue living under the weight of a life that you do not want. You will likely discard this conscious approach to the manifestation process, but you will come back to it later and, in all likelihood, repeat the exact same mistakes. The critical point here is that even though you abandon your vision, you still impress upon the Creative Life Force your doubt, impatience, disappointment and belief that you are powerless to make a difference. The result is that you continue to manifest more of the very thing you are attempting to rise above.

Another critical point is that you cannot use your vision to eliminate the responsibility of using your executive faculties in constructive ways now, within the context of your whole situation. You may say to yourself that your faith will increase when you start seeing results of your vision. This is not true. You are now and always using the full power of your faith. Where your faith is focused is another question. Creating a vision for a new life is invigorating, but take care to not split your life into the future good you desire and present conditions you do not. If you are trying desperately to get away from your circumstances, then it is important to observe the ways in which you are employing your faculties of imagination, faith, judgment, will and elimination. If you could snap your fingers and instantly be in the position that you envision, the chances are good that you would create within that new position conditions identical to the ones you are in now. This would be similar to taking the same play to a different theater.

Enter your daily routine knowing your prototype exists and is coming forth now, but also enter it with mindfulness toward the way in which you are currently using your executive faculties. Do not use them to attempt an escape of your present environment; use them to transform it.

Step 4: *Wait until some circumstance pointing in the desired direction begins to show itself. It may be small, but it is the type and not the magnitude of the circumstance that is important. This is the first sprouting of the seed.*

The beauty of this five-step approach is that it requires you to become attentive to your life as it is now. Nothing new needs to be created. You plant your vision, become receptive and expectant, and then you wait. Be alert to doing things that will make your outer life more reflective of the desires of your heart.

While we look for the full fruit of a desire to appear, we may miss the tiny sprout that ultimately matures into the desired fruit. The manifestation process does not happen outside of you but *through* you, and it nearly always unfolds in ways common to your everyday life.

The feeling of being trapped is the result of the belief that conditions must undergo a complete transformation before you are satisfied, almost as if your life takes place within a concrete prison cell and the only escape is a radical breakout. This fourth step opens your mind to the idea that the apparent walls surrounding you are porous, and that even within these walls opportunities can present themselves and start to make a difference.

One change that can occur within the walls is a shift of attitude that blesses rather than curses your life. If you continue to mull over all the reasons you do not like your life and focus only on what is wrong, you will not see possibilities for making it right. With your mind open to even the smallest of opportunities for manifesting your desire, you create an internal environment that is open and nonresistant to new growth. Your internal environment is based on understanding that your life is unfolding in an orderly way. This understanding sparks the strength and enthusiasm to do the things that need to be done. Sometimes you are called to action and other times you need only continue holding the high watch knowing the Creative Life Force is working through you in meaningful ways.

The advice in this step then is to become observant, to wait rather than force things to happen. If impatience dictates your actions, you must support your manifestations through willful means and this undermines the integrity of the manifestation process.

Step 5: *Do whatever the circumstance seems to require. This action leads to the further unfolding of other circumstances in the same direction. By addressing each one as it appears, you move step by step toward the accomplishment of your desire.*

Again, do not ignore seemingly small opportunities that arise and appear to have little to do with your ultimate goal. Would you not offer shade to a tiny sprout that was getting too much sun? How simple an act and yet how vital to the survival of your plant. You do not have to construct a metal roof and put in a central cooling system. A piece of cheesecloth hung on a pair of twigs might do. Your job is to be observant and ready to respond to even the smallest details of the unfolding of your forthcoming vision. On the other hand, the work you are called to do may require much of your time and attention involving long hours and late nights. It might pull you from your comfort zone and stimulate thinking and actions you didn't realize you were capable of performing.

An opportunity to act on your vision will arise. You perform the action and then nothing more presents itself, or much time passes between opportunities to act and it feels as if nothing is happening. You are tempted to stir up things and force something to happen. But just as a plant experiences spurts of growth and then rest, there are often periods of rest between those times when action is required.

The question of when to act and when to let go and trust is one that has plagued us all at one time or another. There are those who do nothing when something can and should be done. There are others who are so busy doing this or that thing that they take no time for stillness and openness to inner promptings. The secret is to first let go of everything: your desire, your plans, all frantic search for the best method of acquisition. Find a degree of inner stillness and consider your options from this place of peace and power. Examine closely whether your motive is to evolve greater strength or to protect a weakness. A weakness in this case may mean that you are capitulating to impatience, which is nearly always a factor when you find yourself attempting to force things into the impossible service of making you feel better. Examine every aspect of your desire until you are completely clear as to why you are pursuing it.

I'll conclude this chapter with the reminder that I present the proceeding series of steps as a technique that will help you become more aware of your relationship to the ever-active manifestation process and to keep your faculties focused. An important part of implementing any technique is your willingness to identify and release old beliefs that may seem logical but do not work. We'll go into depth on the value of letting go in the next chapter.

–6–

The Power of Letting Go

A healthy state of mind is attained when the thinker
willingly lets go the old thoughts and takes on the new.

—Charles Fillmore
"Renunciation," *The Revealing Word*

These words of Charles Fillmore are especially relevant
when considering how to get what you want from life. Many
people approach this subject with the belief that they need to
accumulate more knowledge or receive something more from
God. If you are among them, perhaps you will find it worth
considering that your answer may lie not in the accumulation
of more information but in letting go of faulty information you
have been using to navigate through your life.

Illustration of a Sponge

If you fill a saucer with water and place a dry sponge in the
saucer, the sponge absorbs the water. Refill the saucer, then
again place the saturated sponge in the saucer. The sponge,
already full, absorbs little or no water. Its relationship to the
water in the saucer has been neutralized. Place the saturated
sponge in an even larger tub of water and the sponge, despite
the greater abundance of water, absorbs no more. Now squeeze

water from the sponge and it will regain its absorbing power. The key to the sponge's ability to absorb is found in its emptiness.

This principle holds true with your consciousness. Examine your beliefs and you will find that you hold many preconceptions formulated on the assumption of your incompleteness rather than on an understanding of your wholeness. This is why you can live and move and have your being in God (Acts 17:28) and still fail to experience this all-sustaining presence. You see yourself as existing in a condition of separation from all that would be comforting and fulfilling. Your personal awareness is so saturated with such preconceptions that you neutralize your relationship with your soul's native environment. The living signals that emanate from your spiritual core translate in your mind as distant, unfulfilled longings. These signals are actually a perpetual beacon of your complete and presently accessible wholeness. Your conviction that life can someday be better is a misunderstanding of what it can be right now.

Though you currently exist in an unrestricted environment, you seem to absorb few if any of its benefits, not because they are inaccessible but because the focus of your attention simply does not permit it. Your field of awareness is so saturated and so preoccupied with the needs and demands of your personal existence that you are unable to see that you already float in all the cosmic energy that will ever be available to you. You have come to accept as a given the belief that you are separate from your spiritual source, that you are incomplete and that with enough effort and training you will one day regain your consciousness of oneness.

How long do you think it will take you to awaken to the presence of God? You may be surprised to find that you have actually worked out a timeline. There is even a good chance that you do not expect to awaken at all. You have tried and failed too many times and you never seem to make any progress. You resign yourself to the notion that you will not attain a satisfying level of spiritual enlightenment now or in the foreseeable future.

The man who, for 38 years, lay by the pool of Beth-zatha (Jn. 5:2-9), near Jerusalem's sheep gate, did not expect to *ever* make it to the healing pool. Jesus, who recognized the healing presence of the Creative Life Force, not in the water but in the man, did not take into consideration the man's indefinite timeline. He invited him to engage present healing energies. "Stand up," said Jesus, "take up your mat and walk" (Jn. 5:8). Jesus did not change the behavior of the Creative Life Force. Within a matter of moments he inspired the man to squeeze the sponge of his belief system and reabsorb the truth of his being.

As I suggested earlier, when seeking to get more from life you may not have considered the importance of letting go of your preconceptions. You want to know what you can do or where you can go to fill your sponge with even more and fresher water. You want to find that perfect tub or that healing pool in which you can place yourself and draw a different, more fulfilling experience. For a sponge that has lost its absorbing power, it matters not whether it is placed in a larger bowl, a pool or an ocean; it can absorb nothing more.

Blocking the Light

Here is another way to think about this problem. Imagine taking an empty jar and setting it in a ray of sunlight. The light passes through, creating only an outline of a shadow. Now imagine filling the jar with smoke. The smoke blocks enough light to cast a complete shadow.

Think of this shadow as your life. You would like more light. Will you ask the sun to give you enough extra light to eliminate the shadow? Or perhaps you could coax the sun into breaking a few orbital laws and moving to a position straight overhead so the shadow will disappear. Neither of these will work. The sun is as bright as it's ever going to be and it's not going to move for you or for anyone else.

When shadows of negativity appear in your life, you may turn to God in prayer asking that they be removed. If you think of God as the sun, you as the jar, the smoke as your consciousness and the shadow as the negativity in your life, you will have an effective understanding of how to approach the problem. You do not ask God to behave differently. God is behaving just fine. You do not try to eliminate the shadow by applying external force to blow it away. You eliminate the smoke from within the jar; that is, you eliminate the internal negativity that is casting the shadow in your external life.

The Hidden Treasure

Nothing is closer to you than your own spiritual essence. Are you failing to experience this expansive level of yourself because you are flawed or incomplete? No, your awareness is so crammed full of misconceptions that you can absorb little more than an intuitive hint of your pure essence. So you must rid yourself of these misconceptions.

Jesus had a number of parables illustrating the act of letting go as the first step toward spiritual understanding. His story of the man who found treasure buried in a field is one of the best.

> The kingdom of heaven is like treasure hidden in a field, which someone found and hid; then in his joy he goes and sells all that he has and buys that field. (Mt. 13:44)

You capture the spiritual significance of this story when you think of the treasure as your native soul and its all-sustaining spiritual environment. The field is your field of awareness. The man discovers the treasure and then hides it, an indication that his ensuing actions are his secret. Your quest for an inner experience is private, something to be kept to yourself. This doesn't mean that you refrain from being involved in a spiritual community or that you cease discussing spiritual issues with others. Only you can go within yourself and find the treasure of your native soul. This is a solo experience that no one can help you with. Teachers can tell you about the treasure they discovered in their own field, but they cannot give you the experience you seek. Only you can make this discovery and engage in the act of acquiring the field. The sooner you understand this, the sooner you learn to trust yourself and trust the notion that your spiritual objective is within your reach and you have the ability to find it.

It is common for students of spiritual studies to think of their spiritual nature as potential in need of development. This perceived development involves the disciplines of study, thought control, limiting exposure to negative influences and increasing exposure to all that is good and true. Over time, according to this approach, the consciousness translates into more spiritually compatible external conditions.

In the parable, however, the treasure is not depicted as potential, as an undeveloped skill or a business opportunity. The treasure is immediately present in its full value, like a chest full of gold. For the man to take possession of the treasure something must first happen. You might think that he needs to accumulate more money, enough to buy the field, but he does not do this. To buy the field he sells what he owns. From a spiritual point of view, there are reasons why this action makes sense. Selling what he already has means the man can take immediate possession of the treasure-bearing field. And judging by his joy, the treasure is worth more than the sum of his possessions. Letting go of things he has valued allows him to acquire something of greater value than all of these things combined.

Compare this to your own approach to spiritual development. It is likely that you think you need to accumulate more knowledge about your native soul before you can gain a working possession of it. This is one example of a false belief that you must sell. Holding this belief causes you to invest your faculties in an idea that is not true. When you touch your innermost being, even for a few moments, you discover that it is different and much more accessible than you thought. You cannot gather facts that accurately describe it or glean new information that will enable you to experience it. Such facts appeal to your logic because you sense they are true, but the acquisition of more information about your spiritual nature does not open the inner gates. You may even boast that you have been studying spiritual principles for 30 years, holding up this long history of apparent devotion to spiritual matters as if this should somehow translate into a title of wisdom or some measure of enlightenment. Only direct apprehension of your native soul entitles you to such a designation.

To capture the significance that the treasure is worth more than the sum of the man's current possessions, you have to consider what is meant by *possessions*. Remember that Jesus is talking about the immediacy and accessibility of the kingdom of God. The possessions that prevent you from entering this kingdom are your misconceptions. You undoubtedly hold many beliefs about this spiritual kingdom that are contrary to its being present and accessible by you now.

A belief, regardless of how strong or well founded, does not contain the power to either augment what is true or enable you to experience it. It simply causes you to use your executive faculties of imagination, faith, judgment, will and elimination in ways that correspond to the belief. There are a number of beliefs you must *sell* (release) and we'll look at some of them in a moment. For now it is enough to say that a belief does not make a thing true or false, it only affects the way you employ your faculties. Senses-based beliefs do not put actual distance between you and the spiritual dimension, but they do alter the way you experience it. I am not implying that all senses-based information is false or useless. I am saying that no information that comes through your senses, either through reading or hearing, has the ability to deepen your connection to your soul. Senses-based knowledge either generates or alters *beliefs*. The intuitive experience that you gain through regular periods of meditation instills *knowing* derived from direct exposure to the spiritual dimension. All belief is based on information gathered through the senses, primarily the eyes and ears. True knowing is imparted through the portal of intuition.

The spiritual experience cannot be obtained through the senses. You can retain volumes of information about the spiritual experience, and you can learn how to assume an intuitively receptive posture, but this information does not constitute living knowledge and transforming experience. It can transform your belief system, and it can change the direction of your thinking overall, but it will not open the intuitive portal of your imagination and expose you to the eternal light of Spirit that you crave.

Emotional Stimulation Is Not Spiritual Conversion

What many refer to as a spiritual conversion is little more than the intellectual and emotional stimulation that comes from exposure to belief-altering ideas. Such exposure is thrilling and somewhat satisfying, but it is only a ripple over the surface of the mind. The intuitive portal remains closed. In our earlier illustration of the digital camera, this would be the equivalent of composing a shot in the viewfinder without clicking the shutter. Many great images can pass through the viewfinder, but at the end of the day you're left with nothing to show. This would be like the man in the parable discovering the treasure, selling his possessions, buying the field and then telling you of his experience. Seeing the man's excitement, you study his life, his treasure and the impact his discovery has had on him. Your mind becomes filled with facts about the man and his life while your own treasure remains hidden. You are to discover your own treasure, to tap into the Eternal that is forever waiting to meet your uplifted vision. Meditation is the single practice that will open your intuitive portal to the Infinite and lead you into a direct experience with this thing you seek.

Many approach Jesus as the man who discovered the treasure. Meister Eckhart offered an insightful bit of wisdom concerning this subject:

> Now one authority says: "God became man, and through that, all the human race has been ennobled and honored. We may well all rejoice over this, that Christ our brother has through his own power gone up above all the choirs of angels and sits at the right hand of the Father." This authority has said well, but really I am not much concerned about this. How would it help me if I had a brother, who was a rich man, if I still remain poor? How would it help me if

I had a brother, who was a wise man, if I still remained a fool? (182)

Eckhart is suggesting that if Jesus is to have any relevance or impact on us, then we must adopt the way demonstrated by him. Doing this requires the discovery of your own treasure rather than gawking in reverence and amazement at his. By his own admission, Jesus had no greater ability than other members of the human family. The thing that set him apart was that he opened the intuitive portal, surpassed our limited, senses-based beliefs and lived from the free level of his native soul.

A point that should not be overlooked in this parable is the fact that the man already owns enough to buy the field. He does not have to work another 10 years to raise the money. He only has to be willing to let go of his possessions. He sells them in joy no doubt because he understands that the value of the treasure exceeds the value of this property.

If you compare this story to your own spiritual journey, you will probably discover some interesting contrasts. For example, unlike the man in the story, you might be laboring toward a treasure you do not understand, one that is based on vague intuitions and the input you glean from books and teachers. You may have a general idea that there is a treasure and that it can somehow make your life better, but you are unclear about what you need to do to come into possession of this treasure.

The parable puts forth a very different scenario. Jesus depicts the man as one who has actually seen the treasure. A great barrier to progress in the spiritual awakening is that you may not have actually seen and experienced the treasure you seek, so you work on speculation. It is nearly impossible to stay with something you are not sure is real. At the first sign of a challenge, you abandon your spiritual notions and employ old methods of handling your life's problems. This is discouraging, for it leaves you with the feeling that your spiritual ideals are far from you, impossible to attain at your current level of understanding.

You Cannot Damage Your Soul

No matter what happens, you cannot damage your native soul and you certainly cannot lose it. Your soul is a treasure that you already literally possess, though not necessarily at the conscious level. You are not months or years away from possessing it, for your native soul exists now as a turnkey operation. You cannot form a strong enough attitude to affect the truth of this relationship one way or the other. Your native soul is no further or closer to you than it has ever been. It is forever the essence of your being.

The general consensus is that the spiritual path is a long and arduous struggle of evolution. But the term *gospel* means "good news." The parable of the treasure clearly reflects the sense of joy and immediacy. Why would Jesus put forth such an ideal if it were not possible to attain? He could have just as easily depicted the man discovering the treasure and then taking 20 years to sell his possessions to buy the field. The good news put forth by this parable is that the treasure is presently accessible and obtainable.

This concept of selling everything is critical, but it is important to understand that it applies to your present accumulation of beliefs rather than material possessions. Like the saturated sponge incapable of absorbing more water, your consciousness is likely full of preconceptions about your spiritual nature. Selling possessions is releasing preconceptions about who you are and what your life means. In the parable, notice the man's joy stems not from letting go, but from his discovery of the treasure. He is motivated by a genuine revelation rather than by intriguing concepts. The treasure is not a theory or a promise that may be fulfilled if he continues to plod along in blind hope of a better future. He has actually seen the treasure. All his actions are based on a thing that is now a real part of his experience. He *knows*.

There is a good chance that you are striving to attain a theoretical spiritual identity you have never experienced, which is why you can never attain it. Is the image you hold of your spiritual nature yours or is it a composite pieced together from books, teachers and your own speculative thought? Have you further distanced yourself from your treasure by making it the exclusive domain of the so-called spiritual giants of the world? Perhaps you can affirm your spiritual heritage without feeling like a blasphemer, but can you affirm it without feeling like a trespasser? The man in the parable, like most of us, discovers the treasure on someone else's land. He then makes the land his own. If you do not make the land your own, you will see it as out of reach because you have not been granted the special blessing of spiritual enlightenment.

Jesus addressed this shift from trespasser to landowner when he explained to Nicodemus that one had to be reborn of spirit to understand the spiritual dimension. Nicodemus assumed Jesus was talking about physical birth. "How can anyone be born after having grown old? Can one enter a second time into the mother's womb and be born?" (Jn. 3:4). Jesus made it clear that he was speaking of a shift in self-perception, that your being emanates from a spiritual source. "No one can enter the kingdom of God without being born of water and Spirit" (Jn. 3:5). Being born of water represents an intellectual cleansing. To be born of spirit is to experience the shift from thinking of yourself as a senses-based identity to knowing your true identity as a spiritual being.

Understanding the Way Shower

We have rightfully designated Jesus as a spiritual *way-shower*. In doing this, however, many have inadvertently accepted the idea that they are perpetually lost. The role of a way-shower is to point you in the right direction so that you may get on your way. Imagine you are looking for a shop in an unfamiliar neighborhood. You stop at a convenience store and ask the clerk for directions. The clerk, who explains that she has been there many times, tells you to go east four blocks, turn left on Third Street, go one more block and you'll see the shop on your right. Suppose you drive one block, become distracted and then forget the rest of her directions. You turn back and ask her again and she gives you the same directions. If you keep repeating this scenario, you will never get to your destination.

The kingdom of God is within you. How many times do we need to have these simple directions repeated? Did our Way Shower not make this clear enough when he said, "I am in the Father and the Father is in me" (Jn. 14:10), and again, "I am going to the Father" (Jn. 14:12)? He didn't say, "Someday I'll be in the Father and the Father will be in me," and "Someday I will be going to the Father." He spoke in present tense. I am in the Father (spiritual Source) and the Father is in me. I am now drawing from my spiritual Source even as we speak. This is the secret behind the things I do and say, the secret that allows you to do what I do and even greater things. You, too, are presently immersed in your spiritual Source and your spiritual Source is immersed in you. Go to this Source now and live from it.

Even with this clear direction, many will say, "Okay, how do I do that? I need someone to show me." It is significant that the man in the parable is alone when he discovers the treasure. You will not find your completed soul in the whirlwind of others' opinions regardless of how well-founded, logical or spiritually correct they are. Yet in all likelihood, it is this impossible group-related search that you are calling your spiritual path. You have mistaken the authoritative opinions of others for the wisdom you seek, opinions that have become your prized possessions of spiritual authority. This is one of the reasons achieving spiritual enlightenment seems so difficult. Year after year you search for something swirling in the whirlwind of other people's thoughts, snatching at this piece of debris and then that one. With each seizure of information, you think you have brought yourself closer to what you are seeking, but still you do not have the treasure. Snatching at flying debris is a tiring process that produces only a momentary lift of hope. This is a version of inspiration, but it is not the divine *breath of the Almighty* that you crave from your living Source.

The way to the treasure you seek is the shortest, least laborious of all. You labor to be more loving and more forgiving and you struggle to have more faith. Your native soul is presently love so vast that it is incapable of harboring ill feelings toward anyone or anything. Nothing threatens its existence. Words like *faith* and *hope* mean nothing to your native soul, which lives in a perpetual state of knowing. While the image-driven personality tells you there are yet four months before the harvest, your native soul invites you to lift your spiritual eyes, to open your intuitive portal and see that the fields are now ready for harvest (Jn. 4:35).

You are working hard to fix an image of yourself that is not fixable. You want to heal it. You want to prosper it. You want to breathe new life into it and gain respect and community status for it. You want it to become flush with feelings of self-worth and confidence. In addition to all of this, you want this self to be spiritually enlightened. In short, you are trying to build a spiritually based, image-driven personality.

Most of us labor to bring forth a spiritual image we have conceived through senses input, a problem that is addressed in these words from Isaiah:

> Why do you spend your money for that which is not bread, and your labor for that which does not satisfy? Listen carefully to me, and eat what is good, and delight yourselves in rich food. (Isa. 55:2)

Think of money as the energy of your attention and you understand the writer's point. Why are you giving your attention to a *concept* of your spirituality, when you can open yourself to the real, the true spiritual dimension that is within you as your core being, your native soul? This Scripture invites the reader to make a new choice for a *present* good that truly satisfies. Think about this. You are working toward an ideal of the spiritually enlightened person you believe you are supposed to become. Where did you get this ideal image? It probably came from reading and listening to others talk about it. Having read and listened and given much thought to the subject, you pieced together this picture toward which you aspire. In holding this image of your hoped-for future attainment, consider also the image you hold of your current spiritual status. Because you hold an image of yourself as someday being more advanced, more complete, you also entertain a self-image that is spiritually incomplete. You cannot hold one without holding the other.

You are never going to achieve an image-driven, spiritually enlightened personality, nor do you need to. All that you are trying to build has already been built, and it is so secure that concepts of *death* and *limitation* are of no consequence. Conversely, the self you are working so hard to perfect still shudders with the slightest change in the breeze. No matter how many stakes and guy wires you install, this image-driven personality is a flimsy structure, a tarpaulin shelter next to the stone castle of your native soul built to withstand the ages.

The possessions you have to sell are beliefs, and the following 12 are among the most common.

1. My spiritual nature is potential to be developed.

Your spiritual nature is already fully developed. Your work is to create an environment of consciousness that is compatible with and receptive to this truth. Start with the idea that you are complete, that your native soul is fully present and accessible to you now.

If you hold the thought that your spiritual nature is potential, you will forever say, "I am *here* and spiritual enlightenment is *there*." Begin now to affirm that your fully enlightened native soul is as present as it will ever be and it is shining into the field of your awareness.

2. More study will bring me closer to my spiritual nature.

The point of spiritual study is to align your consciousness with the Truth stated in the first item. More study does not bring you closer to something that is already the foundation of your being. Learning more facts about your spiritual nature will not open the intuitive portal of your imagination and let in the light of Spirit. Albert Einstein, a towering intellect, made this statement: "Much reading after a certain age diverts the mind from its creative pursuits. Any man who reads too much and uses his own brain too little falls into lazy habits of thinking, just as the man who spends too much time in the theaters is apt to be content with living vicariously instead of living his own life" (qtd. in *Twelve Powers* 87-88).

What many consider their spiritual quest is little more than a vicarious stimulation of ideas generated from the minds of others. Their search is not yet directed within themselves. They justify this by citing the credentials, the apparent brilliance and the large following of the teachers they admire.

3. Negative thinking and negative attitudes put distance between me and my spiritual nature.

In the literal sense this is not possible. Your thinking may make you miserable, it may put you in a mental and emotional space where you feel completely separated from your Source, but it never puts your spiritual nature out of reach and it cannot cause damage to that which is eternal.

In the parable of the prodigal son, the father's love for his wayward child never wavered. The boy's home was always present and available to him despite the fact that this youth's logic told him that his poor judgment had likely compromised his standing in his father's household. Upon his return, the father honored his son with a joyous celebration. In the father's mind, the boy's standing was never in question.

How you see yourself determines how you think of yourself. You can change the way you think about yourself, but if you do not capture the true vision of your native soul, any improvements you make in your thinking will be temporary. Jesus illustrated this dynamic in yet another parable:

> When the unclean spirit [the body-based identity] has gone out of a person, it wanders through water-less regions looking for a resting place, but it finds none. Then it says, 'I will return to my house from which I came.' When it comes, it finds it empty, swept and put in order. Then it goes and it brings

> along seven other spirits more evil than itself, and
> they enter and live there; and the last state of that
> person is worse than the first. (Mt. 12:43-45)

You can forcefully sweep your house (consciousness) of the demon of low self-esteem, but without the power given by spiritual vision it is only a matter of time before this demon returns with its friends: failure, futility, feelings of spiritual incompetence and the countless other demons that result in a spiritually disconnected, senses-based identity. It is this identity, not your spiritual essence, that is occupied by these demons of limitation. While they ransack your mental and emotional house, your spiritual identity remains untouched, as if you are looking down from a loft that is inaccessible to these marauding invaders.

4. Positive thinking brings me closer to my spiritual nature.

This is not possible. While positive thinking enables you to accomplish many things, spiritual enlightenment is not one of them.

> For my thoughts are not your thoughts, nor are
> your ways my ways, says the Lord. For as the
> heavens are higher than the earth, so are my ways
> higher than your ways and my thoughts than your
> thoughts. (Isa. 55:8-9)

There is much confusion around the idea of what constitutes a positive thought. Positive thinking is associated with optimism toward some type of accomplishment. Optimism and positive thinking are indeed important components of a life of accomplishments. On the spiritual quest, however, a positive thought is something much more than a "can do" attitude toward an accomplishment. A positive thought is one that is charged with the vision of the pristine region of your native soul. Positive thinking, in its highest and natural form, does not begin with a concern for accomplishing things in the outer world. It bubbles forth from the aspect of your being where all things are already accomplished. True positive thoughts are the children of your native soul. Touching your inner depths will do more to influence your thinking in a genuinely positive way than any association with even the most highly charged positive thinkers in the world.

Positive thinking is a natural effect of the spiritual awakening. The thoughts generated are not contrived but true and in complete harmony with your spiritual nature. Notice the man in the parable of the hidden treasure became joyous *after* he found the treasure. His is not drummed up optimism designed to improve the quality of his life. His joy is the spontaneous effect of making this unexpected discovery.

The thinking generated by instructions to be positive is often a senses-based activity that will take you no higher than the intellectual level. The prodigal son could have affirmed that his life in a foreign land—starvation, sharing the food he fed the swine, being alone—was a wonderful, character-building experience, even a lesson given by God. In that low moment his highest thought was to return home as a servant so he could eat better. What if he had only attained his highest thought? Compared to the actual reception his father prepared, his willingness to work as a mere servant would have been a much degraded experience.

That which you seek is beyond your best thinking, beyond the highest emotional experience you can generate. Of course you want to live your life with a good attitude, but let it be an attitude stimulated by the discovery of your inner treasure, a true joy that rises from an authentic experience of your native soul.

5. My thoughts are my reality.

This statement would indicate that there are multiple realities and that each person's universe of thought is a separate one. There is but one Reality. Your thoughts create an illusion of reality. To call the product of your thinking *reality* ties you to a false notion equivalent to an earth-centered universe that has nothing to do with what is true of the larger cosmos. People who make the claim that their thoughts are their reality are often seeking justification for erroneous thinking. "I'm speaking from my truth," they may say, as if *my truth* is Truth. The product of your thinking is simply that—the product of your thinking. The highest thought you can generate does not come close to the spiritual experience you seek. The spiritual experience will, however, generate thoughts that you will not otherwise have. You will never find your native soul among your thoughts or among the thoughts of others, regardless of how enlightened they appear. These are but moonbeams in comparison to the full power of the sun.

6. God can either be patient or impatient with me.

This cannot be true. God is changeless and does not express different moods that are affected by your attitudes or behavior. "For he makes his sun rise on the evil and on the good, and sends rain on the righteous and on the unrighteous" (Mt. 5:45). You cannot provoke God to anger, impatience, sadness, disappointment or cause God to act in ways that are vengeful, unloving or withholding in any way. Nor can you do things that will earn God's favor. These are all human attitudes we have given to the Creative Life Force and to labor under any of them is to create an unnecessary burden. Nothing you do or fail to do can cause God to behave differently. You are either in alignment with or in opposition to the behavior of God. To align yourself with God you must first understand that which you are aligning with. Direct experience rather than contrived behavior or thought brings you into alignment with the true activity of God.

7. My current lack of understanding makes me unworthy to experience my spiritual nature.

It is fairly safe to assume that the apostle Paul lacked understanding of the teachings of Jesus when he experienced his conversion on the road to Damascus. That your spiritual nature can break through at a moment's notice is also profoundly illustrated in cases of near-death experience. You may be thinking that a spiritual experience comes as the result of much practice, like taking up piano. You would not consider the possibility of making your debut at Carnegie Hall in just a few short weeks. Spiritual awareness, on the other hand, can break through at any moment. Based, no doubt, on his own spiritual awakening, Paul wrote, "We shall all be changed, in a moment, in the twinkling of an eye" (1 Cor. 15:51-52 RSV).

8. I must completely silence my mind to experience the highest truth.

My most profound spiritual experience came one evening when I was completely frustrated with God. Yes, opening yourself in silence to your deeper being is an important discipline. Just bear in mind that it is your openness to Spirit that ultimately allows it entrance into your awareness. If your time of silence feels like a struggling game of hide and seek, you may actually be enhancing the illusion of distance between your current awareness and what you want to experience. "Listen! I am standing at the door, knocking; if you hear my voice and open the door, I will come in to you and eat with you, and you with me" (Rev. 3:20).

9. I must fix myself before I become enlightened.

One of the most difficult ideas for people to grasp is that at the spiritual level there is nothing wrong with them, nothing that needs fixing. Nor is there a need to fix your senses-based identity. You don't fix it, you discard it—or, more accurately, you allow it to be absorbed into your whole identity. As the personality assumes its rightful role as a function of your native soul, it rights itself in a way that is far more efficient and effective than you can achieve with even the best set of instructions. This work of fixing yourself is not yours to do. Your job is to open yourself to the completed work of Spirit in you.

10. I must be more loving toward others if I expect God to be more loving toward me.

Again, whether or not you love, God is love and God is completely unable to veer from this unchanging truth. Love is not a thing that God does, an action God takes. Love is a characteristic of God. Love is the quality that remains when all myth and illusion surrounding God are dispelled.

Many think of love like a container of gold dust that they carry about and distribute or withhold according to the worthiness of those who come into their sphere of influence. We reason that this one is a good person who deserves some of our gold, and that one is not, so we withhold our treasure. If you *try* to love, you are not loving. Like the warmth produced by your body, love is a naturally radiated expression of your unhindered being.

11. I must forgive before I am forgiven by God.

Yes, I know what Jesus said about forgiveness. God, however, does not forgive because God cannot condemn. When you forgive, you release yourself from the prison created by your own condemnation. God has never inhabited this prison. In the same way, you cannot find light among shadows, you cannot find anything in God that even remotely resembles condemnation.

It really is this simple.

12. My soul is of a lesser quality or stature than that of Jesus and others who I perceive as spiritual giants.

If this were true, why would any spiritual teacher waste their time talking to the so-called common people? What would be the point? Though the scale of understanding is wide, everyone, from the spiritual genius to the spiritually inept, is of the same species. What the spiritual genius expresses is equally accessible to the spiritually inept. The greatest teachers *want* to guide you to the kind of experience they are having. They know that discovery of your own soul marks the end of your search and the beginning of a more meaningful experience.

–7–

The Role of Choice

Jesus was a master at drawing examples from common elements to illustrate abstract spiritual principles. His acute awareness of the spiritual dimension caused him to see these principles illustrated in the most ordinary aspects of nature—lilies, seeds, sunshine and rain—and through industries common to his region—farming, fishing and raising livestock. He then used these common elements to link spiritual concepts to the human experience. The people who heard him speak were struck with his wisdom. "How is it that this man has learning, when he has never studied?" (Jn. 7:15). Today people still speculate on the sources of his knowledge. Some suggest he studied with little known esoteric groups. Some New Thought circles attribute his insight to being an old, highly evolved soul. The Christian traditionalist claims he was the only son of God. Still others make the case for his traveling to the Far East to study among mountain dwelling ascetics.

To think that we would have to travel to uncover the mysteries of Omnipresence or to study under others to gain understanding of our own soul is to undermine or miss entirely the truth that our connection to God is an inner one. Jesus drew universal wisdom from the indigenous well of his native soul.

Those who fail to grasp this, fail to grasp the accessibility of their own inner well and are destined to wander in vain looking for a spiritual prize. Jesus was not unique in his capacity to know God; he was unique in his choice to devote himself to doing so.

It is our ability to make choices that has brought each of us to our current place in life. Jesus seemed to understand this on a much deeper level than most. In one notable parable, for example, he used the very mundane task of sorting a day's catch of fish to illustrate the role of choice as it pertains to the spiritual awakening:

> The kingdom of heaven is like a net that was thrown into the sea and caught fish of every kind; when it was full, they drew it ashore, sat down, and put the good into baskets but threw out the bad. (Mt. 13:47-48)

When placed in the context of ideas we have considered thus far, the message becomes immediately useful. The ability to choose plays an important role in the process of aligning your consciousness with your soul. The net represents your mind and its ability to gather ideas, the fish of every kind. Remember that your faculty of imagination has the dual capacity for receiving ideas both intellectually (through the senses) and intuitively (from within). The most common understanding of the imagination is that of its image-making ability. Most of our imagery is based on information drawn from senses input, much of which is quite useful for practical invention and for everyday communication. The vehicle you drive, the machine you use to wash your dishes, and the house you live in are all products of the inventive side of the imagination. Even conversation with the friend at the grocery store is full of imagery generated by this brief exchange of words.

As interest in your spiritual nature increases, you discover that your inventive imagination, only sporadically grounded in the changeless spiritual dimension, creates at least as many problems as it solves. The idea of intuition itself may seem an ambiguous concept, seen as little more than the occasional hunch that asserts itself in unexpected times. Without the guidance provided by the intuitive portal opened to your native soul, you see that you have reached many wrong conclusions about who and what you are. As the intuitive portal opens, you begin making choices at all levels that support the furtherance of your spiritual awakening.

In the parable, the workers sit down and sort the fish. The standard used to distinguish between good and bad is determined by the fisherman. If the fishermen intend to sell their catch as food, they make a certain choice. If the catch is going to a science lab, they make a different choice. The fishermen represent your executive faculty of *judgment*, the choice maker. The fish are the multitude of ideas that swim through your mind. Some swim close to the surface and others are found in the deep. When you close your eyes to meditate, you are immediately confronted with fish that inhabit the surface waters. If you are seeking to understand spiritual principles so you can create conditions to make your personality look and feel better, you will chase after these surface-dwelling fish. If you are seeking a deeper understanding and experience of your native soul, you will bypass these and go for the fish that inhabit the deep. Your choice-making process is tied directly to the way you define yourself.

From the cosmic point of view, there are no good fish or bad fish, just fish. Likewise, there is no cosmic standard for good or bad ideas. The standard is set by you. If your intention is spiritual discovery but you pursue every kind of idea that happens to flitter through your mind, your spiritual journey will be long and laborious. Nothing in your life is going to change until you change the type of ideas you pursue. The more direct experience you have with your native soul, which is a choice you make, the more value you place on inviting it to the forefront of your daily thought.

Emotion Does Not Equal Experience

Because it is easier to *think* about spiritual things than it is to experience them, many make the mistake of believing they are drawing fish from the depths when they are really drawing them from the surface. You spend an hour reading and thinking about spiritual things and in this hour you experience a warm place of peace and hope that you recall fondly throughout your day. Or someone sends you an email containing beautiful pictures and words of a spiritual nature that gives you a lift. A beautiful thought about the spiritual dimension, even when it stirs a pleasing emotional response, should not be confused with a direct experience of your native soul. Thinking about and feeling good about spiritual things is not the equivalent of experiencing them. You could read many books about apples, for example, and you could think all day about what you have read. This does not compare to what you gain by taking a single bite from an apple. Just as the taste and texture of the apple instantly changes the way you think of an apple, a moment of pure experience with your soul changes the way you think of your spiritual endeavor.

There is a common error that says specific types of thinking generate an experience of the deeper reality. The reverse is actually true. Remember Emma Curtis Hopkins' statement from the introduction: "For it is primarily what we most see [experience from inner visioning], and not what we most think, that constitutes our presence, power and history." A single glimpse of your native soul changes what you think.

Trace your dominant thought stream back to its source and you will find the headwaters issue from the vision you hold of the person you believe you can and should become. Further reflection will show that you hold this vision because you believe you are incomplete. This is a false image, but it is, in all likelihood, the one that controls the way you employ your faculties, judgment in particular. You exercise judgment that is in keeping with your current self-perception. Your real work is to discover the reality, the real *you* behind this false image. You think you need to change yourself and your life conditions, but in truth you only need to agree to move into the deeper reality that is the source of your being. Trying to change your thinking before releasing this inadequate self-image is like attempting to make an aquarium fish as appealing to the palate as it is to the eye. It cannot be done.

It may come as a shock to realize you are attempting to accomplish a goal of self-improvement that you can never achieve. The image you are working toward represents a composite of senses-based information that is, in all likelihood, anchored in a mass of ideas gleaned not from the headwaters of your native soul but from others. Based on this information, you have created the goal toward which you labor. As long as you hold an improved self-image as a future possibility, you simultaneously hold the image of yourself as inadequate and incomplete. You are, in effect, a house divided.

Let's take this a step further. Some people hold a vision of a future humanity as more spiritually enlightened, that the human family will one day live in tune with the principles of love and harmony perceived as the ideal. Some claim that within our lifetime we will see this dawning of a new age of mass spiritual enlightenment. This, in fact, is an ancient hope that is resurrected from time to time, usually when the future of humanity appears to be in jeopardy. All biblical apocalyptic writings are examples of this perception. The view of a brighter spiritual future reflects a severe misunderstanding of present-moment Reality that causes its followers to look to the future for salvation that exists only in the present. Jesus addressed just this point of view: "The kingdom of God is not coming with things that can be observed; nor will they say, 'Look, here it is!' or 'There it is!' For, in fact, the kingdom of God is among you" (Lk. 17:20-21).

Though you are capable of quickly making the shift mentioned by Jesus, as long as you hold a futuristic vision of a better world you are not likely to see the better world that has always been here. Why? Because it goes against everything you have accepted as true concerning your spiritual development. Why did a man like Jesus ask his listeners, "Do you not say, 'Four months more and then the harvest'? I tell you, open your eyes and look at the fields! They are ripe for harvest" (Jn. 4:35). What eyes and what fields do you suppose he was talking about? He referred to the spiritual eyes, the intuitive portal of the human imagination. The fields ready for harvest are your completed soul which you do not see because your judgment has been blinded by futuristic thinking. You have become so fixated on visions of greater good yet to come that you do not see the depths and beauty of the reality that, as the Gospel of Thomas says, *is spread out upon the earth, and people don't see it* (Miller 303).

Nor did Jesus say *work* on letting your light shine or take more classes or read more books or get a better paying job or heal your mind and body first so you can let your light shine.

He did not suggest going out and doing good deeds or becoming an upstanding citizen or a social activist so all could see the goodness and selfless service you render to the much improved world you intend to establish. He said *let* your light shine. Your light is present. You may lift the obstruction of spiritual misinformation and let it shine now.

As we have seen, there are two ways to gather information. The most common is that of observing external conditions and pondering facts gleaned from these observations. We refer to this type of information as *sense perception* because it is drawn through the five senses. This may include information of a spiritual nature. The second method of information gathering involves turning within and observing intuitively the inner working of the Creative Life Force in the native environment of your soul. The externally directed method of information gathering produces intellectual enlightenment. The second internally directed method of information gathering results in spiritual enlightenment. Intellectual enlightenment definitely has its place, for it goes a long way toward improving the human condition. Retaining facts about the spiritual dimension should not, however, be confused with spiritual enlightenment.

In this book, for example, I am sharing insights I have discovered from going within myself—with the understanding that you have your own spiritual center, your own native soul from which to draw knowledge and instruction. To share my insights, I must convert them into intellectual information, which I pass from my intellect to yours. You cannot, however, experience your native soul vicariously through the information I share, nor can I live the experience you might share with me. We can exchange words, but we cannot exchange experience.

The so-called *hundredth monkey effect* applies to the intellectual exchange of information. It does not and cannot apply to the spiritual awakening. Senses-based ideas can be passed from one intellect to another resulting in a collective "awakening" to the benefits of that idea. The spiritual experience cannot be passed from one mind to another. The only way the individual can experience the spiritual dimension is from within.

Just as this long-awaited kingdom was within the people Jesus addressed, it exists in its fullness within every person today. Likewise, the kingdom he spoke of as being present then is equally present now. Nothing new from the outside is going to come into your life and bring you peace and harmony. Nothing new is going to be introduced to the inhabitants of the world to cause them to create a utopian society. The entire mechanism for all we seek, individually and collectively, is in place now and has always been in place. Ironically, the choice to believe in a better world to come is the very choice that keeps the hoped-for world eternally out of reach.

Many find this distinction between intuitive and intellectual knowing confusing. Most of what we associate with intellectual enlightenment and the material advancement of civilization we attribute to the exchange of ideas between minds. The utilization of electricity, for example, was spread in this way. This ability to pass on ideas does not apply to the spiritual awakening or, as I've already indicated, to the so-called spiritual advancement of the species. Spreading ideas about the spiritual dimension is not synonymous with individuals awakening to their divinity.

Many religions are driven by the need to "spread the word of God." What they mean is they want to win as many converts as possible to a certain way of thinking, to bolster their denomination with numbers and money. Unfortunately, this enormous undertaking does not translate into spiritual enlightenment for the individual convert. On the spiritual course, each person must learn to navigate from their own intuitively stimulated experience. The insights thus derived are entirely different from those taken in through the ears and eyes and processed by the brain. Their effect is for a purpose completely different from that normally associated with intellectual illumination. The goal of intellectual development is grounded in self-improvement, the improvement of conditions or simply the stimulation of learning something new. In contrast, the goal of spiritual enlightenment is to awaken to the completeness of your native soul, an experience of supreme joy. The life conditions that follow in this wake take care of themselves.

To illustrate the difference in these two types of illumination, imagine putting a light source inside a box, covering it with a lid and placing it in a dark room. Though there is a brightly shining internal light source, the box is lost in darkness. Turn on a spotlight and you light up the box. Turn on more spotlights and you brighten the box even more. But turn off the lights and the box returns to darkness. Cut holes in each side of the box so the inner light may escape. Now you can move the box into the darkest corner of the room and there will be light.

I once received a phone call from a man who explained that he had been living under a bridge when his mother gave him a copy of one of my books. He said he could not remember exactly what in that book triggered it, but "all the lights flashed on." He went on to explain that he suddenly *knew* the power that could change his life was within him, that this deeper force had awakened, that he became charged with a knowing that enabled him to leave his life under the bridge and step into two different kinds of work he loved, one of which included racing cars. The thing that impressed me most was the fact that he could not remember a specific helpful point in my book. My words had simply served as the catalyst that helped him connect with his own inner light. If this connection had not been made, he might have read the book, tossed it and continued living under the bridge.

In another instance, I received a letter from a man who told me he had been on the verge of taking his own life. He had written his suicide note and had counted out the pills he intended to take to overdose himself. He said he just happened to have his radio on and heard my broadcast. In that desperate moment, something I had said seized his attention. He connected with his inner light and this gave him the strength to move through his crisis.

In both cases, these men were intelligent and capable, but somehow their head knowledge had become disconnected from their inner light. The intellect that is illumined by outside information depends on a steady supply of such information to feel complete. Many see the process of meditation as a time of reading and contemplating the works of others, of basking in the light they cast. Study is preparatory to illumination: you study to understand that the inner light is present. However, contemplating the thoughts of others is not the type of meditation that awakens you to your native soul. Through study you understand that your inner light is present. Meditation is the process of opening your intuitive portal to this "light [that] shines in the darkness, and the darkness did not overcome it" (Jn. 1:5). The intensity of this inner light does not increase through study, nor does it decrease through ignorance of its presence, as illustrated in both of the above-mentioned cases. It is as bright now as it will ever be. Like these two men, your work is to come to experience its self-existent, self-sustaining presence as the core of your being. Your attention in this direction opens your intuitive portal and lets out the light that you are.

As you consider this ability to turn in one of these two directions for your source of information, you are, of course, focusing on your executive faculty of *judgment* in its highest possible role. When you take the spiritual approach to getting what you want from life, it is critical to distinguish between the sources from which you draw ideas. As a rule, all you read and hear of a spiritual nature is a product of sense perception, information that comes to you from external sources, the spotlights that illumine the outside of the box. You read words from a book or hear them spoken by a teacher. The information enters your consciousness through your eyes and ears and you process it by making comparisons with what you have accepted or rejected as true. Following this method, you expect to develop the condition of spiritual enlightenment. While externally gathered ideas do illuminate the intellect, you will not reach a condition of spiritual enlightenment by accumulating even great quantities of information about your spiritual nature. Too much information may postpone your awakening.

This does not mean that all externally oriented information, either conveyed through a book or a speaker, is false. As a writer, I do my best to convey ideas that are true, but I understand the limitations involved in communication. All inspiration, all mental or emotional stimulation produced by external sources should *not* be mistaken for the spiritual awakening you seek. If, after years of exposure to spiritual ideas, your life seems to be no better, the problem is not in the ideas gleaned from others but rather in your belief that the spiritual awakening can be obtained from an outside authority. The senses-based logic that most people rely on to deal with practical matters becomes a hindrance when applied to the spiritual awakening.

Opening the intuitive portal marks the beginning of an entirely new experience of spiritual awareness. Most people accept that a span of time must pass before their faculties and understanding mature enough to handle spiritual illumination. As you actually open this inner portal, you see the fallacy in the belief in a long and laborious process of adding to your mind layer upon layer of information of a spiritual nature.

> Ask, and it will be given you; search, and you will find; knock, and the door will be opened for you. For everyone who asks receives, and everyone who searches finds, and for everyone who knocks, the door will be opened. Is there anyone among you who, if your child asks for bread, will give a stone? Or if the child asks for a fish, will give a snake? (Mt. 7:7-10)

These passages make it clear that if you are earnest in your spiritual quest, you will find the awakening you seek. If you seek and do not find, it is probably because you are looking through the conglomeration of ideas you have gleaned from others. The inspiration derived from ideas makes you feel like you are on the path. These are simply signs pointing to the path. The path itself is a living center of energy that you know the moment you touch it. Notice that Jesus does not say that only some who seek will find, while others will not, or that the door will be opened to the few and closed to the rest. The reason that people, like Jesus, make these all-inclusive statements is because he was on this path and he knew that it was accessible to all. You can succeed in touching it.

Charles Fillmore started his spiritual quest in the same way most of us do. He studied the works of a number of teachers, so much so that he became quite confused about their many seem-ingly contradictory statements. He later admitted that he was inclined to ridicule those making spiritual claims. But he did what we all can and must do. He turned directly to God.

> I said to myself, "In this babel I will go to headquar-ters. If I am Spirit and this God they talk so much about is Spirit, we can somehow communicate, or this whole thing is a fraud."

> I then commenced sitting in the silence every night at a certain hour and tried to get in touch with God. There was no enthusiasm about it; no soul desire, but a cold calculating business method. I was there on time every night and tried in all conceivable ways to realize that my mind was in touch with Supreme Mind. (qtd. in Freeman)

In time he began to find what he had been seeking. One can argue that he had something more than the average person, that his soul was advanced or that he was sent by God to do the spiritual work we know as Unity. Charles Fillmore was an ordi-nary man with little formal education, living a normal life sup-porting a family through buying and selling real estate. To say he was something more or different than others misses the point that each of us is one with the Creative Life Force and, should we make the choice to do so, are capable of experiencing conscious unity with our Source.

Though this relationship of unity and wholeness exists, we are so occupied with events and concerns connected with the maintenance of our bodies, minds and surroundings that we have made God a distant concept that is far from our reach. Throughout history, theologians have placed God in the sky or on mountains or in the inner sanctums of a temple, places that were either literally inaccessible or deemed off-limits to the average person. It is a sad fact that the orthodoxy of most religions is steeped in a conceptualized version of God that is far removed from reality. In contrast, the mystics, often within the framework of these religions, speak of God as an inner experience. In all times, those sensitive to the spiritual dimension have recognized this cosmic ocean washes equally over every person. Some have embarked on this sea, some have taught the music of the surf, some have spent their lives building dogmatic sand castles and some have slept beneath umbrellas. Those who have embarked upon these living waters have attempted to awaken others with the message that the things they see can be seen by all, a message that has been missed entirely by the majority of the human race.

The spiritual concepts you glean do not contribute to your already developed soul. Thus far you have compared your progress to others in your spiritual community and gauged your growth in terms of the quantity and quality of books you read and teachers you have sat before. These things have no bearing whatsoever on who and what you are. They remind you of the truth of your being, but they may also encourage you to continue seeing yourself as spiritually underdeveloped. The moment you touch even the hem of the garment of your native soul, your spiritual journey takes an entirely new and authoritative turn. You understand that your work does not lie in developing your spiritual nature but in bringing forth its fully developed character to the forefront of your consciousness. You do this by making the choices to let go of ideas that are incompatible with the truth you experience firsthand.

The intuitive aspect of your imagination becomes the inlet into your field of awareness for the living energy of your soul. Your faith is no longer bolstered by what you read or hear but by what you experience from your authentic depths. You exercise your power of judgment, not according to theory or ideas put forth by others, but by a spiritual standard that has become a real experience to you. Your faculty of elimination, formerly used to deny the appearance of evil, is now turned to releasing those elements of your senses-based identity that place you at the mercy of negative appearances.

You may understand that appearances can be misleading. The effectiveness of this understanding, however, has nothing to do with holding an affirmative mental attitude intended to alter or possibly dissolve the appearance. *True affirmation involves a shift in the point from which you are looking, not a shift in what you are looking at.* Viewing a situation from your senses-based identity causes the situation to appear a certain way. Looking at the same situation from your spiritual depths allows you to see it in another way. If you continue to view an appearance from your senses-based identity, the use of denials and affirmations will prove to be little more than an exercise in mental gymnastics. There are times when these gymnastics seem to actually alter appearances. You go through your litany of statements, conditions change and you think you have had success. The next time you apply your denials and affirmations nothing changes. You muster more willpower and double your efforts, but to no avail. You conclude that you do not know enough or that maybe you might have introduced a negative thought or perhaps you need a whole new set of denials and affirmations.

The key is not found in the employment of new, more powerful words or some different technique provided by yet another spiritual teacher. The key is to let go of ideas that keep your awareness riveted to untruths. In other words, denial becomes a releasing of *where* you are in consciousness at a given moment. You shift from a dweller in your senses-based identity to that of your spiritual completeness. Again, denials and affirmations have nothing to do with altering appearances. They have to do only with altering the position from which you view appearances. When you view an appearance from the position of your senses-based identity it looks one way; when viewed from the position of your native soul it looks another. Toss the fish that keep you attached to your senses-based identity and keep the fish that are compatible with your native soul.

Acquiring more information about the spiritual quest is not as useful or as impactful as direct exposure to your completed soul. In terms of influencing your judgment, one moment of experience with the sweetness of your soul is worth more than all the ideas contained in hundreds of books. What some think of as spiritual knowledge is often little more than information about spiritual things. Scholars, attempting to explain how a person of insight has reached their conclusions, trace the lineage of their thought-stream in search of the sources that they believe first produced the notion. These intellectuals cannot conceive of the possibility of individuals drawing from an original fountain of intelligence. The true mystic draws directly from the source of all wisdom. That their message sounds like others that preceded them is explained by the fact that they have visited similar terrain.

Again, that which constitutes an authentic spiritual awakening cannot be transmitted from one mind to another. What is transmitted is inspiration, not experience. Inspiration occurs when you receive ideas that are compatible with your native soul and these ideas momentarily open the circuit that allows the light of your soul to penetrate your awareness. With enough of these, you reason, you will accumulate the light you seek. Think of these inspirational ideas as a pinhole in a piece of black construction paper. Each tiny hole allows a minute amount of sunlight to pass through. Poke more holes in the paper and you will get more sunlight.

In contrast, remove the paper altogether. You see that even a thousand pinholes are as nothing in the full radiance of the sun. In the same way the full strength of the sun cannot be experienced through even a large number of pinholes, the spiritual awakening does not come from years of accumulating ideas. It comes with dissolving the veil of false beliefs that stand between your mind and your soul.

I encourage you to get in the habit of using often the statements included in the introduction:

My completed soul is now radiating light.
I am conscious of this light.

Approach your time of quiet introspection with the expectation that your completed soul knows how to emerge through the intuitive portal into your consciousness and is doing so now.

-8-

An Evolution of Values

In the previous chapter we examined the role of choice-making and the impact it has on our spiritual awakening. In this chapter I will put forth the idea that we make specific types of choices because of the values we hold. When I refer to *values,* I am referring to those things that you believe you must have to get what you want from life. Your values, as we will see, are directly related to the manner in which you define yourself.

Let's say you have arrived at the place where you understand the value of awakening to your spiritual essence, and you understand how a practice like meditation will benefit you in this awakening. You close your eyes with the intention of opening your mind to the radiant light of your soul. You find, however, that your mind immediately fills with trivial thoughts. It is as if you are on a journey with a specific destination and you encounter a swift river that you need to cross. You wade into the water, but the current is too strong and, by all appearances, you can go no further. What do you do? You sit on the river bank and you contemplate your situation. How important is it to cross this river? Your answer depends on the value you place on your objective beyond the river.

Now suppose there is a tree on the opposite bank and nailed to that tree is a tiny slip of paper. With a pair of binoculars you can see this is no ordinary slip of paper. It is a winning lottery ticket worth 100 million dollars—*with your name on it*. Would you conclude that the river is too swift and walk away from the problem? Not likely. Why? You would not walk away because you understand the value of 100 million dollars. You would figure out how to cross that river.

Experience is the key to evolving your system of values. You understand the value of money because you have experienced what it can do. Your understanding of the benefits of a spiritual awakening, on the other hand, may be entirely speculative, based on information provided by others rather than actual experience. This information is good as far as it goes, but it will not satisfy your spiritual craving. The time comes when you realize that such input, enlightened as it may be, can take you no further than the river bank. You read. You are inspired. You close your eyes and you encounter this seemingly impassible current of brain chatter. You spend the time attempting to halt this incessant thinking by affirming something or returning to something you read and memorized. When your "quiet time" is over, you go about your daily activities from the same side of the river.

If this coming to and going from the river bank represents the extent of your so-called spiritual experience, you may conclude that you are still spiritually immature, that you require more years of repeating this cycle before you can ford the river. You have already mastered the art of coming to the river bank and more practice will make you no better at it. If you were not spiritually mature enough to cross now, you would not even have considered this river of incessant thinking as a problem.

Those who are spiritually asleep consider this river a normal aspect of the landscape. What is all this fuss about forging it?

The truth is you are capable of moving beyond this river of mind chatter. You will not do it, however, until you truly grasp the value of doing so. How do you reach this point? You observe your repeating pattern of arriving and turning away and you realize that more of the same will get you no further along. Teachers and books, you see, present you with ideas you already know. All that remains is for you to cross.

You begin in earnest to study the river and the problem of getting to the other side. Only then will you notice that there is a rope—moss-covered and nearly invisible—lying beneath the water's surface. You grab this rope and begin to pull yourself across. Your hands may slip and you may swallow some water, even turn around and come back. But if you stay with it, you will make it across and you will have a firsthand experience with your native soul. This, you know, will represent a milestone, a major departure from your old attitudes toward spiritual matters.

A Shift in Values

Many people operate under the false belief that breaking through the incessant thought-stream is itself a destination; once this place is reached they will forever rest in bliss. Spiritual exploration is no different than the exploration of space. Both are infinite and neither offers an ultimate destination, a permanent stopping place. Landing on the moon has been a crowning achievement, but no one involved in space exploration sees the moon as an ultimate destination. In 1996 and again in 2004, scientists pointed the Hubble space telescope into areas of space that appeared to be devoid of stars. The 1996 experiment, which held Hubble's camera shutter open for 10 days, produced an image of more than 3,000 galaxies, each containing hundreds of billions of stars. Using further refined equipment, the 2004 11-day exposure produced an image containing more than 10,000 galaxies. The image, known as the Ultra Deep Field, represents the farthest we have ever peered into space. With each discovery we answer a handful of questions and raise a million more.

Likewise, there are no stopping places in our exploration of the spiritual dimension. Reaching the other side of your incessant thought-stream is not an ultimate destination. It is, however, a major breakthrough that affects the way you define yourself in relation to your spiritual Source. This breakthrough represents the commencement of a new set of values grounded in the direct experience of your native soul. You shift from seeing yourself as incomplete to actually knowing your completeness. The false belief that you are incomplete and that the spiritual journey is about becoming more complete has caused you to adhere to a certain set of values. The direct knowledge of your spiritual completeness causes you to shift to a different set of values.

In the Sermon on the Mount, Jesus offered important advice pertaining to this issue of values and how they tie in directly with our self-image:

> Do not store up for yourselves treasures on earth, where moth and rust consume and where thieves break in and steal; but store up for yourselves treasures in heaven, where neither moth nor rust consumes and where thieves do not break in and steal. For where your treasure is, there your heart will be also. (Mt. 6:19-21)

Treasures on earth are those things the senses-based identity believes will make our self-image complete. These perceived treasures are not confined to material items. As we have seen, they can also include such things as your spiritual studies. In these studies, you are seeking knowledge that you hope will fill an inner void and make you feel complete. Through your studies you accumulate inspiring ideas that change your thinking in a positive way because they make you feel better, at least momentarily. The experience of feeling better should not be confused with the experience of having touched your spiritual completeness. Your treasure trove of positive ideas and catchphrases is not immune to being stolen by that master thief we all know as *fear*.

There is a major difference between the pursuit of things that protect you from fear and attracting things as the result of uncovering that part of you that genuinely knows no fear. Though Jesus is directing attention to the latter, few seem to grasp this distinction. The root of all fear is grounded in the perception that you are incomplete. This false perception becomes the basis of a value system that actually steers you away from the very fulfillment you seek. The word *heart*, as Jesus uses it in the earlier passage, is your *passion*. When you are passionate about something, you bring all the forces of your being into focus in a single direction. Where your treasure is, there your passion will be also. When you place a high value on discovering your perfect inner light, when it becomes the primary object of your study and quiet time, the light you seek will dawn. You will experience the breakthrough that you seek.

Limitless Energy

Classical Newtonian physics states that a certain amount of energy must be applied to set an object in motion. The greater the energy applied, the greater the motion that follows. According to this logic, you may believe that you must work hard to sustain a positive attitude and keep your focus on spiritual matters. Your soul, however, does not adhere to Newtonian physics but operates under a different set of rules. You are sustained by a perpetual energy source that is never depleted. In a conversation with a Samaritan woman at the public well, Jesus spoke of this energy as a spring of water:

> Jesus said to her, "Everyone who drinks of this water will be thirsty again, but those who drink of the water that I will give them will never be thirsty. The water that I will give will become in them a spring of water gushing up to eternal life." The woman said to him, "Sir, give me this water, so that I may never be thirsty or have to keep coming here to draw water." (Jn. 4:13-15)

Because of the apparent waxing and waning of your feelings associated with your spiritual endeavor, you may find it difficult to grasp the concept of a nondepleting energy source. Some days you feel high with spiritual energy, some days not. There is a simple way to illustrate that this energy is operating around and through you at all times. Take a pair of scissors and snip a single blade of grass from your lawn. The part of the grass that remains rooted in the soil heals and will grow back to its original size in about a week. Clip 10 blades and you will see they recover their original size in the same amount of time. Mow your entire lawn and you will see the exact same recovery period. If you and everyone in your town mow their lawns, there will still be no difference in the recovery period. Now imagine everyone in the world mowing their lawns at the same time. Think of the amount of energy required to return all these trillions of blades of grass to their original condition. Yet the recovery period for all the grass will remain consistent. Were it possible to coordinate such an experiment, we would see that this phenomenal demand would not lessen the availability of the required intelligence or healing energy one iota.

Unlike the grass, the senses-based identity requires constant renewal of energy. It has to constantly seek out new sources of inspiration to keep it propped up. Your native soul, on the other hand, is sustained by the same energy that grows all the flora and fauna on the planet. Regardless of how many living things there are, the energy and intelligence that sustain each one does not wane. The increase in the human population alone would represent a substantial draw on the Creative Life Force, yet the increased number does not deplete the spiritual energy available to each.

We are used to thinking of our soul as an electric light that dims when the air conditioner comes on. The native soul never dims. In contrast, the senses-based identity waxes and wanes constantly, for it draws its energy not from an infinite source but from external elements that are exposed to moth and rust and subject to change. When there is plenty, the senses-based identity experiences peace of mind. When there is scarcity, or even the suggestion of scarcity, peace appears to evaporate. More effort on your part, you reason, is needed to correct conditions that bring more peace. In contrast to this thinking, have you ever prayed that your grass will recover after having mowed your lawn? Do you feel the need to visualize for every blade a renewal to its original stature? Of course not. You accept as a given that the energy to heal and revitalize each blade of grass is present and at work and you have no doubt that you'll be mowing again next week. You apply one value system to your grass and another to your soul. Jesus suggested that you merge these two value systems:

> But if God so clothes the grass of the field, which is alive today and tomorrow is thrown into the oven, will he not much more clothe you—you of little faith? (Mt. 6:30)

When you come to understand that your soul is supplied in a way similar to the grass in all the lawns and fields in the world, you begin to see the meaning of eternal life, that it is not an indefinable length of time but a self-perpetuating, non-depleting process. To grasp the presence of this self-perpetuating energy underlying your soul is to gain eternal life.

The Wealthy Young Man Revisited

A great lesson in values is found in another story involving Jesus and a wealthy young man. The young man approached Jesus and asked,

> "Teacher, what good deed must I do, to have eternal life?" And he said to him, "Why do you ask me about what is good? One there is who is good. If you would enter life, keep the commandments." He said to him, "Which?" And Jesus said, "You shall not kill, You shall not commit adultery, You shall not steal, You shall not bear false witness, Honor your father and mother, and, You shall love your neighbor as yourself." The young man said to him, "All these I have observed; what do I still lack?" Jesus said to him, "If you would be perfect, go, sell what you possess and give to the poor, and you will have treasure in heaven; and come, follow me." When the young man heard this he went away

sorrowful; for he had great possessions. (Mt. 19:16-22 RSV).

The young man, wealthy and morally upright, still feels something is missing. He wants to know what he can *do* to feel his oneness with God. What social cause can he join? What charity can he contribute to? What good thing can he do for the planet that will help deepen his awareness and make him feel better about himself? It is interesting that Jesus shoots back to him the pat answers that every Jew had been taught since childhood. If this exchange had taken place in a modern New Thought context, Jesus might have said, "Study, make sure you tithe, spend time daily meditating on spiritual ideals, pray often, go green, memorize affirmations and above all keep a positive attitude." Like many today, the young man had performed all these things, but it was not enough. Jesus' ultimate response amounted to a complete shift in values. "If you want to experience your connection with God, let go of your belief that external acts will bring you what you seek. Turn within, make this spiritual connection your highest priority and you will make the breakthrough you seek."

Let's put this story in a slightly different context. Imagine a famous swimming champion standing on a beach. A young man clutching a large bag of rocks that he has collected for landscaping purposes approaches the swim champion and says, "I want to learn how to swim like you." The swim champion, sensing the man's attachment to the rocks, assumes he is simply seeking instruction and he gives a few pointers. The man explains that he already knows swimming theory. He would like personal instruction from a champion. The swim champ says, "Great. Drop your bag of rocks and follow me into the water." The man says, "But I've spent all morning collecting these rocks. I have a special place for each one in my yard. These are important to me and I don't want to risk someone taking them while we're out swimming." The swim champion says, "Well, you can't swim *and* cling to your bag of rocks, so you have to decide which you want to do." Still clinging to his rocks, the man turns away saddened that he must forgo the opportunity to swim with a champion.

Both of these stories illustrate the conflict that exists in many who are trying to reconcile their spirituality with the fact that they are expressing in a material world and have material needs. Most of us, like the young man, try to advance spiritually while maintaining, as our priority, a materialistic, senses-based value system. The secret of finding balance is to cultivate awareness of the spiritual source from which you arise. The value system of the young man was morally upstanding, but still something vital was missing. Jesus advised him to sell what he had, give the money to the poor and then follow him. This advice represented such a complete shift in the young man's value system that he could not make the change.

A Test of Values

If you accept that your native soul exists in its completed form now, you have to ask yourself why you cannot seem to experience it. When you sit down to become still and you find your mind darting off to resolve this or that issue, you are, at that moment, placing greater value on chasing after these things than on experiencing your soul. Instinctively you know that your soul is of much greater value than these frivolous pursuits. Still, you have to accept that you are placing more value on the shifting interests of your undisciplined mind than on cultivating a deeper experience of your soul. You can argue that these things demand your attention, as if you have no choice in the matter. What you do with your mind, however, is a choice only you can make. You are making choices because you see some value in the process of running after thoughts, even though you know they will never come to anything.

This river of incessant and frivolous thinking does not exist as a power standing between you and your depths. It is more like the water hose that has flown from the grasp of the fireman, undirected, spewing wildly over everything but the fire. While it is true that you have harnessed your mind's power to the point where you can set and accomplish certain goals, your native soul requires more than your passing attention.

When I was a boy, one of our family cats, Pepper, would go out into a field and come back with mice, frogs and small snakes. She would bring these to the door and meow to be let in so she could proudly show off her offerings. No one, my mother in particular, wanted mice, frogs and especially snakes let loose in our house. Like Pepper, you are laying the gifts of your accomplishments at the feet of your soul, seeking its nod of satisfying approval. Your soul smiles and praises you for what you have done and then turns away from your offerings. Your soul is no snob. The problem is that nothing you bring is large enough or freeing enough to satisfy it. You are offering gifts of clothing that are too small and do not fit. Your soul would rather you stop bringing things to the door and bring yourself instead. Only you have the capacity to satisfy your soul. Your being is the garment that fits and allows your soul to express all the beauty and splendor that it is.

When you say, "let thy will be done," the chances are good that you are thinking of turning things over to the unpredictable actions of a foreign god. Address your native soul as "thy" and offer your whole being with all your faculties as the agent of expression. Your being is the means through which you express the fullness of your soul on this planet and you require all your faculties to succeed in this endeavor.

Deep longing, dissatisfaction and unhappiness are signals from the most powerful force you will ever encounter—your very own native soul. These are calls for a complete remaking of your system of values. Your soul is nudging you to give up the things you currently value, and turn your attention to your spiritual awakening.

You cannot and will not abandon the pursuits on which you place high value. You let go of them only after you discover something of greater value. The man that discovered the treasure buried in the field had spent all his life accumulating possessions that he obviously valued, otherwise he would not have put forth the energy to acquire them. When he discovered the treasure in the field, he knew immediately that he had discovered something that was of more value than all his possessions. He did not force this determination—he came to it willingly and joyously. Nothing more is being asked of you.

Jesus did not condemn the wealthy young man for rejecting his advice. He knew the man, accustomed to attaining things to support his senses-based identity, had not reached a place where the experience of his native soul had become the objective of highest importance. The young man was looking at eternal life as a thing he could purchase, either with money or with service. He wanted to add something more to the trove of possessions that would make him feel more complete. The thought of divesting himself of his power source, his possessions, was repugnant, a foreign concept that had no value to him.

I Was Here!

There is also the possibility that this young man was seeking eternal life for his senses-based identity. It is not unusual to see people of wealth seek a type of immortality by leaving an edifice that marks their passage on this planet. Giving their names to streets, buildings, foundations or notable institutions or programs is a way of saying, "I was here! See all the good deeds I have done. Don't forget me!" In some cases their motivation could be the fear of total annihilation. They draw a measure of comfort from knowing that when they are gone others will remember them and, perhaps, think fondly of them for the good they leave behind.

Many throw themselves into charity work with similar ambition. They may not advertise their contributions but they believe that selfless service to the "underprivileged" will earn them a special place in God's kingdom. Charities themselves play on this idea by presenting service as the Christian thing to do. Even in this selfless behavior you are bringing a mouse to the door of your soul. Losing the ego in service to others is not the same thing as offering your being as the exclusive outlet to your native soul. The value in contributing to charity, especially when the service requires your physical presence, is that it prompts you to think about something other than yourself and the senses-based orbit you occupy. Doing deeds that make you feel good, however, does not translate into soul discovery. You can lose yourself in service to others and this may feel freeing for a time, but it does not fulfill the requirements of soul awareness and expression. Mother Teresa provides one of the best examples of this loss. To the world, she was the epitome of selfless service. Her personal spiritual life was apparently an empty void. "As for me," she wrote to the Rev. Michael Van

Der Peet, "the silence and the emptiness is so great that I look and do not see, listen and do not hear" (Van Biema).

You do not find yourself by losing yourself in service to others. The greatest service you can render to your fellow beings is to offer yourself to the will and workings of your native soul. Your soul will instruct you by direct impartation.

A Contrast Worth Noting

There is a contrast worth noting between the story of the wealthy young man and the parable of the buried treasure. The man who discovered the treasure sold all he had in joy. The man seeking eternal life found the thought of selling his possessions depressing. The difference is that the man who was willing to sell his possessions had *seen* the treasure, while the wealthy young man had not. One was responding to an experience; the other was responding to sense perception.

When you awaken to this inner fountain, even briefly, it literally takes possession of you. You will experience it and you will lose it, you will experience it again and you will lose it again, but you will never forget it. So pure and sweet is this inner life that once you get a glimpse of it nothing less will measure up. You will discern which presentations of spiritual ideas are authentic and which are simply information passed on at the intellectual level. You may follow some of these lesser teachings for a time, but you will find they quickly lose their luster. Once you awaken to the spiritual dimension, you will know from that moment on where to find the source of living water for which you thirst. The man who discovered the buried treasure represents this shift from theory to knowing.

The wealthy young man was engaged in performances—following rules and doing good deeds—that he believed would bring him the highest prize, eternal life. Yet his efforts did not earn him the thing he was looking for. He approached Jesus for more instructions that would give him satisfying results. Compare this scion of privilege to the man who stumbled upon the treasure. There is no hint that the man in Jesus' parable had been working on himself to do the right things to earn the treasure he found. Once he found it, he began doing the things needed to acquire it. His ensuing method of acquisition was given to him, not by others who wrote or spoke of the treasure, but by the treasure itself.

Taught by God

To be taught by God simply means that your methods of spiritual alignment become dictated by intuitive revelation rather than by input from others. When you see the light for yourself, you know the direction to take. To think that you have to build up your faculties over years of study to perceive this light is erroneous and is the cause of the long and arduous road that so many believe will end at the gate of spiritual enlightenment. H. Emilie Cady was blunt on this topic:

> If you are one who seeks and expects to get any realizing knowledge of spiritual things through argument or reasoning, no matter how scholarly your attainments or how great you are in worldly wisdom, you are a failure in spiritual understanding. You are attempting an utter impossibility—that of crowding the Infinite into the quart measure of your own intellectual capacity. (27)

However, Cady's bluntness is tempered with advice:

> If you want to make rapid progress in growth toward spiritual understanding, stop reading many books. They only give you someone's opinion about

> Truth, or a sort of history of the author's experience in seeking Truth. What you want is revelation of Truth in your own soul, and that will never come through the reading of many books. (28)

This advice, of course, will seem an irony to be included in a book. Yet it needs to be reiterated because it is said so rarely. People have lost faith in their own abilities. We are in the habit of turning to experts before turning to our own innate wisdom. We ask others how to raise our children, how to dress, how to wear our hair, how to act, how to think and how to pray. Living in the information age has its plusses, but one of them is not necessarily a strengthening of trust in ourselves. We make up our mind after running to the Internet, which means we haven't made up our mind at all. We've simply found information with which we can agree.

At a young age I found Cady's book. My soul leapt with joy, for her words resonated deep within my being. And yet that which I sought could not be gained even from many readings of the book. It stirred images of the sea, so to speak, evoking the sound of rushing waves and the smell of salty air, but it did not and could not set me down in the warm surf of spiritual reality.

Like many, I had accumulated a substantial wealth of ideas about my spiritual nature, but I was still not experiencing it. Mere inspiration from yet another idea was no longer satisfying. I craved the experience of the spiritual dimension and I began in earnest to make the inner connection real. I had to lay aside all preconceptions, even my newly acquired ones, and turn within the best way I knew. When I began to open the intuitive portal, I realized the actual light was different than anything I had imagined.

I began to notice that not all authors of so-called spiritually based material wrote from an equal understanding. Some advocated changing one's life by changing one's thinking, but it became clear that they were writing only from a mental perspective, not from clear knowledge of the spiritual dimension. Once I experienced this dimension, I recognized others who had touched it as well. There are authors who write about spiritual things from experience, and there are those who write of a land they have never visited. Still, they have much to offer those of us who value most an improvement of life through positive attitudes. This mental approach, however, falls short of assisting those who have come to the mystical quest not for the purpose of turning poor conditions into better, but with a pure motive for self-knowledge and understanding. The person on this path has reached a point of departure. Authors and teachers of every kind, as primary sources of learning, are left in favor of the inner teacher, the Spirit of truth spoken of by Jesus (Jn. 16:13) as that which emerges from within and teaches all things.

Leave Your Body of Beliefs

Most of us, upon awakening in the morning, begin immediately surveying our material domain. The mind fills with thoughts of the upcoming day, what we will do and at what time we will do it. Memories of yesterday present themselves and we either let them go as finished or plan our follow-up in whatever issues they entail. We get out of bed and go through our normal routine, the whole time thinking about what we will do or what we have done or what we want or do not want within the material realm. We recall favorite spiritually based texts, and we commit ourselves to implementing the ideas as they apply to the acquisition of the things we desire.

The important consideration is your understanding of the spiritual dimension, specifically its relation to your kingdom of material conditions. You want to tap into a higher dimension that will allow a balancing and prospering influence to flood your world. The spiritual call, however, is to leave this world altogether. By this I do not mean that you are to walk away from your life or exit your body. You are to leave the body of beliefs from which you have viewed your life, to redirect the focus of your attention.

If you are like most people, you sweep your attention like a spotlight over circumstances and spend much time reacting to what you see. There are fleeting moments when you turn to the spiritual and live briefly from that ever-renewing fountain of energy you recognize as your native soul. But old habits are difficult to break. You move your attention away from your soul, *which you perceive as the soul receding.* In this seeming low spiritual tide, you feel as if the soul is fleeing your touch—an impossibility. The soul must be approached on its terms. If, in your thought, it is still a thing to be possessed, the time will come when you will understand that you belong to your soul. Attempt to throw your arms around the sea at high tide and see if you can keep it from receding. It will not work. It is the fixed position of your attention that makes the sea appear to run from you. Rather than immersing yourself in the sea and moving with the natural tide, you lock on to a perception, the tide recedes and you believe it has fled.

In your evolution of values, you become less concerned about what you want the Spirit of truth to teach you and more concerned about how the Spirit of truth wants to express through you. Rather than awakening in the morning and surveying your material domain, you awaken to your invisible companion whose presence you know as your sure guide and gentle advisor. You do not call up an invisible guiding spirit that you imagine as dropping reminders here and there that it is leading you to a better life. Your openness to this living presence *is* the better life. As you lay in bed contemplating your day, you do so in the sweet atmosphere of love and light, of knowing that the beauty and stillness that blanket you in this early quiet time have brought you into the morning of a new and beautiful life.

Separating Events From Experience

Events in your life are one thing; how you experience them is something else entirely. The event is the thing that happens. Your reaction to the event is your experience. Most events are out of your control, but you always have control over how you experience them. In this chapter we'll explore the difference between events and experience, and consider ways that this understanding can help you get what you want from life.

You may find this distinction easy to grasp in theory yet not so easy to implement in practice. The more aware you become of the difference between an event and the inner experience you have, the more you understand what it means to be in the world but not of it. The world that you are in is the world of events. To be of this world is to have your inner experience dictated by the ever-shifting landscape of appearances. To be in this world of appearances but not of it is to draw your experience from the ever-present life, power, love and intelligence of your native soul. To overcome the world is to reach that point where you draw a genuine, peace-filled experience from within, even while your world of events appears chaotic.

As your understanding of your life in the spiritual context deepens, making this distinction between events and experience becomes clear. Getting what you want from life means you are looking for an improved quality of life. Logic tells you that you must seize control over the way events transpire. You strive for those events that ensure a high-quality experience. However, because you do not always have the power to decide which events transpire, it becomes vital to your quality of life to know that a better experience does not have to begin with the creation of better events.

Right now there is probably a situation in your life that you would rather not have. Examine your attitude toward this situation. Have you been looking at it and wondering how to change it so you can feel better? Is the event dictating your internal experience, coercing you to think and feel a certain way? Because it looks bad, do you believe you have an obligation to feel bad?

If you are like most people, your logic is going to tell you that if you make a bad situation better, you are going to feel better. Is it possible to genuinely feel better even before the situation takes a turn for the better? In other words, is it possible to change your quality of experience for the better, even though the event remains the same? The answer is *yes*, you can, and you start by detaching your internal experience from the external situation.

As a simple demonstration, think of this bad event and see it resolving itself. Begin entertaining the notion that new, unexpected doors are opening that put the event in an entirely new perspective; you don't have to know how. Think of the event as if you are handing it over to a superior intelligence that knows all things, that knows how to easily resolve this problem in wonderful ways that work for the highest good of you and others. As you consider the possibility of a productive resolution to this situation, notice that new feelings immediately spring up. Your experience, if even for a moment, changes.

Consider now how much more powerful this exercise will be if, rather than just making a mental substitution of ideas, you actually *know* that new doors are opening, that a superior intelligence is resolving your problem in wonderful ways. The practice of spiritual receptivity through meditation acquaints you firsthand with the underlying intelligence that is the basis of your eternal nature. This practice enables you to assume a point of view that allows you to experience events from an entirely new perspective. It is possible to participate in an undesirable event without it forcing you into a negative mental and emotional experience.

You have the choice as to how you will experience events, and this choice-making is a key ingredient to raising your quality of life. You label events as good or bad, desirable or undesirable. If you are unaware of your spiritual nature, you respond according to the labels you have given to events. You become happy during "good" events and distressed during "bad" events. From this point of view, changing your experience still depends on changing events. If you want to experience "happy," you must manufacture "good" events and eliminate "bad" events. However, there is a fundamental problem with this logic. "Bad" events are part of life on earth. If you need to eliminate all "bad" events from your life before you can be fulfilled, you may as well join those looking for the second coming. You're going to be waiting a long time.

Consider verse seven from Psalm 138:

> Though I walk in the midst of trouble, you preserve
> me against the wrath of my enemies; you stretch out
> your hand, and your right hand delivers me.

In this Scripture, walking in the midst of trouble is the bad event. Deliverance from the wrath of enemies is the desired experience. We allow events to control our experience because we are conditioned to treat them as reality. If we are to be realistic, we reason, we must respond to the event in a realistic way. The psalmist, however, points to deliverance *while* walking in the midst of trouble. Deliverance comes from detaching from the event and drawing your experience from your inner being. Even while walking in the midst of trouble you may experience deliverance. The secret is to stop trying to change the event and change instead your response to the event. *You do not need deliverance from the event; you need deliverance from your response.*

How can you experience this deliverance? How can you raise the quality of your internal experience? Spend time alone, closing off sensory input and opening your intuitive portal to the direct impulses of your native soul. Take care that you do not confuse the opening of the intuitive portal with those occasional insights about people and conditions that flash into your mind. These insights may be valid and fit the intuitive definition of instinctive knowing, but they are still *information* about people and things rather than the experience of direct impartations of your soul. It is the practice of meditation that develops the ability to receive the finer impulses of the soul.

Meditation is most effective when, in a quiet state of relaxation, you acknowledge the existence of your completed soul, and you open your mind to its naturally radiating influence. This natural radiation seems foreign only because the mind is conditioned to draw the bulk of input through the five senses. You sense the presence of your soul in the forms of inspiration (the knowledge that you are more) and aspiration (the desire to express more), but because you derive the majority of your experience from senses-based input, these inner impulses are easily eclipsed. In theory you may consider them valid, but you place more trust in what your senses report and less in these intuitive impulses. However, the more you intentionally expose yourself to your soul during meditation, the more you trust and follow it.

Prior to experiencing your native soul, you define your life based on what you see, hear, touch, taste and smell. However, near-death research reveals that even when the heart and brain functions cease and all five senses shut down, you still experience your soul. In other words, nothing that is senses-related, nothing in the material world, has the power to prevent you from having an exalted experience.

Consciously reconnecting with your wholeness eliminates your feeling of weakness and your sense of being lost. This changes the way you interact with events because it moves you from a place of weakness to your point of inner strength. This shift does not necessarily alter events; it alters the way you *experience* events. Because you place yourself in a very different relationship with your surroundings, the choices you make from this point of strength influence the way events unfold. From this vantage point, you quietly evolve a plan of action based on your spiritual strength, rather than reacting to conditions out of fear and emotional weakness. Your entire attitude lights up and you see the world around you in a completely new way. You have essentially overcome the world of appearances.

When you open your intuitive portal, you are choosing to draw your perspective-defining experience from your soul rather than from your five senses. Reality, you begin to know, is not that continuous barrage of information that comes from the outside, but that subtle and persistent power that rises from within you. Of course you continue to employ your five senses, but you draw your experience from the eternal, giving your senses-based input an entirely new meaning. When your experience is derived solely from your senses, you see beauty and goodness only in those places that you have been conditioned to see as beautiful and good. When your perspective is derived from a direct experience of your soul, you see beauty everywhere because you see *from* the beauty and goodness in which your soul perpetually exists. You then bring this gift of beauty to the events of your life.

A number of years ago, I presented a three-day seminar at a Unity event held on the New Jersey coast. When the retreat was over, my wife and I went to stay with a friend for a few days. We had never been to New York City and, though we were close, had not planned on going into the city. From all the negative press we'd been exposed to, we had little desire to do so. When our friend suggested seeing the city by tour bus, we were apprehensive but open to the idea. Apprehension increased dramatically when she dropped us off at a commuter bus stop in New Jersey, sending us on our own into the heart of New York. When I first stepped on that bus and stood looking at all the people, I felt like I was staring into the stone cold face of a city that did not care. Everything in me wanted to turn around and leave, but we made our way to some empty seats without so much as a glance of acknowledgment from our new traveling companions.

By the end of the day we had seen a fair portion of the city, seen that it was not as cold and dangerous as we had thought and we wanted to return. For two more days our friend would drop us off at the bus stop, we would commute into the city and experience more of the people and the sights and in the evening we would return to the stop where our friend would pick us up. In that short period we both developed a warm feeling for the city. In contrast to that moment of first stepping on the bus, on our final trip out I struck up a wonderful conversation with the man seated next to me. The entire bus, in fact, seemed to be filled with an entirely different kind of people. The people, of course, did not change. We were able to let go of the negative preconceptions that we carried to New York. This shift in our inner experience allowed us to see beauty, kindness and wonder in a place where we expected to see little or none.

The quest for agreeable senses-based input is, for many, a primary motivator for amassing wealth. Money provides a great deal of flexibility in choosing the type of senses input you receive. If your region is besieged by clouds, you may buy a plane ticket and in a relatively short period of time find yourself relaxing on a sunny beach.

This type of flexibility does not, however, give you the power to experience the ultimate input from your soul. Money and the desire for beautiful things and surroundings may actually become a detractor to the soul. A reliance on money to alter your inner experience weakens your innate creativity to the point where you stop drawing from this inner well altogether. You do not like the senses input you are receiving, so you purchase new scenes for input or you hire some expert to fix input that is disturbing or you buy new cosmetic input so that you will feel better when you look in the mirror.

Some even believe they can obtain the spiritual experience with money. They travel halfway around the world to sit at the feet of a spiritual master. This is only another purchased event of senses input that ultimately turns out to be just as shallow and temporary in its effects as any other. The ego says, "See what I have done! I have traveled far and studied under this wise master, so consider me wise." Those who attempt to derive wisdom in such a way understand better than any that they are no wiser or no more spiritually connected for their journey. The event may produce fond memories, but traveling great distances brings them no closer to the prize they seek. If you are asleep to your soul in one part of the world, you will remain asleep to it in another.

If you believe that having enough money to purchase whatever kind of senses input you desire will make you happy, then you will do well to observe that people of means are often just as unhappy as those who struggle to make ends meet. There is as much unhappiness and dysfunction among the wealthy as there is among the poor. The wealthy simply purchase a way to mask it. Nothing you can purchase is capable of producing the deep-level soul experience you crave. In light of the spiritual awakening, the playing field is level. Regardless of their economic condition, every individual possesses the means to move into a richer, spiritual experience. What is the means? Emma Curtis Hopkins pointed it out: "We have only one thing to give, namely, our attention"(31). The only thing it costs is your letting go of the incessant mental pursuit of everything under the sun and opening yourself to the rising activity of the Creative Life Force at the center of your being. This is a level of experience that the groping mind, regardless of financial status, can never have.

Your soul is a formless essence often compared to light. We draw this comparison to light because we do not have the vocabulary to adequately describe the soul. Those exposed to this spiritual energy speak of it as the simultaneous experience of absolute joy, peace and beauty. No observable light on earth produces this kind of experience. The soft yellow light of a sunrise over your lawn, for example, might draw your attention, but the scene evokes little more than a few pleasant feelings. In contrast, the light described by the spiritually awakened or the near-death experiencer seizes their attention in a way that permanently changes their perception of reality. There are no senses-based correlations to this type of experience, and those who try to describe it qualify their attempts by stating it is unlike anything they have seen with the physical eye. Some have described it as having the intensity of a thousand suns, yet looking at it causes no discomfort. If looking at our single sun causes discomfort, how could looking at something a thousand times brighter cause no discomfort? Nothing in the realm of the senses comes close to resembling what these people attempt to describe. Yet this same light is the essence of every person's being, yours included, and is, therefore, equally accessible to all with no exception.

The average person is not influenced by this omnipresent light because they are drawing their experience exclusively from sensory data. The soul is effectively buried beneath externally generated information that is mistaken for the real. Reality does not consist of a chain of events or a series of thoughts strung together like beads; nor is it more present or of a higher quality one moment than another. Reality is consistently pleasing to the point of evoking ecstasy at any moment and under any circumstance that you perceive it. The wondrous fact is that we all have the capacity to open our minds to this level—*always*. The only thing that prevents us from doing so is our habit of looking out rather than looking in.

Meekness and Humility

The dispositions of meekness and humility are often associated with a spiritual awakening. These receptive attitudes allow you to move past your attachments to all you think is real, all you think is beautiful, all you think is right, all you think is just, and all you think is true. These attitudes enable you to expand your method of gaining knowledge. You shift from thinking of yourself as a senses-based entity who gathers information simply through the avenue of the five senses to a Spirit-based being whose essence contains more knowledge than all the information humanity has amassed since we first began our inquiry into the nature of the world around us. You see the wisdom conveyed in these words of Jesus:

> Very truly, I tell you, unless a grain of wheat falls
> into the earth and dies, it remains just a single grain;
> but if it dies, it bears much fruit. (Jn. 12:24)

That which must die is your senses-based identity. Dying to this identity and opening yourself to the ever-expanding influence of your soul is the action that will produce the fruit of experience you vainly seek from the realm of events.

We live in a world that lumps together terms like *information* and *knowledge.* Information is not knowledge in the spiritual sense. True knowledge is the understanding that allows your native soul to emerge into the field of your awareness. Concepts derived from limited senses-based information serve you in addressing the tasks of daily living. In the course of a day, however, you become so absorbed in external activities that you develop spiritual near-sightedness and lose awareness of your eternal base. At this surface level you tie yourself in knots hanging on to what you believe is true. Direct exposure to your native soul unties the knots. You move from *believing* to *knowing,* from what is logical to the senses to what is true of Spirit. The senses are not denied but are retrained and invigorated with a life that elevates them to new levels of functionality. They are no longer a one-way inlet for materially-based information but an outlet through which your spiritual essence is radiated to the world. When your vision is born of your inner depths, you no longer see beauty haphazardly. You see it everywhere because you see *from* the inner beauty of your soul.

Your senses-based logic tells you that the spiritual dimension is accessible only to those who have spent years developing their powers of concentration and control of their mind. Omnipresence means that the spiritual dimension is present and accessible to even the busiest, most distracted mind. The apostle Paul was not seeking a cosmic connection while on the road to Damascus. Trained in the tradition of the Pharisee, he assumed that he had obtained enough scriptural facts to justify his destructive actions of arresting and disrupting the lives of the followers of Jesus. He was absolutely set on inflicting misery on those he considered a threat to his well-ordered collection of religious facts. Yet he experienced a level of illumination that resulted in an immediate and permanent change of mind. So deeply profound was this illumination that overnight he became one of the most enthusiastic and energetic proponents of the very belief system he was bent on eradicating.

I pointed out earlier that prior to their near-death experience, many people had no particular interest in spiritual matters, nothing beyond the typical kind of religious exposure common to most. Yet they often come back from these episodes with a view of themselves that echoes the vision of the mystic. Like Paul, most are left confused by the sudden unveiling of the spiritual dimension. The mystic, on the other hand, slowly conditions him or herself and intentionally cultivates this awareness. Even so, in the moment of illumination words fail them.

You have to be ready and willing to move beyond your preconceptions of the way Spirit is to work through you. An inner receptivity and openness to direct experience with the Creative Life Force operating on its own terms is all that is required.

There is no need to give up your current pursuits and blindly turn yourself over to a force that you fear will thrust you into a completely foreign life. You become willing simply to lay aside all conditions that you hope to have fulfilled and prostrate yourself before the inner altar in complete humility, meekness and receptivity.

The spiritual dimension is not located in a specific place; it is everywhere. You are completely immersed in it now. It is the underlying support for all aspects of the visible universe, specifically, your life. What the near-death experiencer and the mystic describe is within your reach. The belief that you are separated from the spiritual dimension by space, time or a lack of knowledge or the absence of a keen intellect is the fallacy that will keep you from experiencing it. It is not the accumulation of additional facts that enables you to awaken to your soul. A willingness to release false, senses-based information and make yourself receptive to this fully present dimension gives it the freedom to radiate through your conscious mind and out into your world.

The general sense of unhappiness that many suffer is merely a symptom of soul suppression. On the one hand, we want events that are going to make us happy, and on the other hand, we know the temporary nature of this stimulation. The soul exists in a perpetual state of happiness, but it is not the type of happiness generated by the possession of things. It is the happiness of cosmic harmony and complete absence of lack or of resistance of any kind.

In the spiritual context, the term *cosmic* does not imply vast amounts of space and time. The cosmic dimension is the underlying Light, the Creative Life Force that is the generating power behind all we see. This force is active in and as you. You are a point of awareness in the Creative Life Force with as much right as any to its healing and quickening qualities. You experience the universal in a conscious and meaningful way by letting go of all that is unlike it. You can only know what this means by directly observing its activity in and as you. As we have seen, when you draw experience from your inner depths, the external aspect of your life is naturally and positively influenced. True peace and power are derived from the limitless resource of your soul. You observe events from the richness of your inner light and wisdom. This becomes your point of strength, an unending fountain of inspiration that knows no boundaries and sees no obstacles.

As you become a firsthand observer of the Creative Life Force, your mind will naturally and joyously conform to its rules. You see that the purest levels of the world's scriptures speak of the perpetually available inner beauty. Your morals are naturally elevated by your desire to experience and express more of the emerging inner light that it may touch others in the profoundly transforming way that it touches you. Rather than attempting to gain control over events, you will pay more attention to the quality of your inner experience. We will see in the following chapter that your expanded inner experience broadens your vision, enabling you to see deeper, more meaningful levels in all the events of your life.

–10–

The Vision Dynamic

Ho you envision your relationship with the realm of events has everything to do with how you will relate to it. It is fair to say that most of us believe the visible realm contains the things that will complete us. We spend a great deal of time and effort looking to the visible for these missing and elusive elements. In this quest for completion, we are likely to think that getting what we want from life is the process of being directed to material success, which increases our stature and makes us feel complete with the least amount of effort. If, on the other hand, you see yourself as a spiritual being that is already complete and you think of the material realm as offering opportunities to reflect your completeness, you will have a very different relationship with the material dimension. Many are convinced that the world is in dire need of change. Spiritual discernment reveals that the world as we see it is simply a reflection of the vision we carry. In your quiet time, observe the part of you that is chasing after things, even spiritual enlightenment, and stop the chase. Incessant thinking is only you running after a state of being that you fail to see as already present as you now. Let your awakening spirit change your vision and you will be amazed by how different the world appears.

Some years ago, my wife and I took our two children on a vacation to the Grand Canyon. The wide view from the rim was breathtaking, and we spent most of a day thrilled to take it in from all the many different vantage points. When we discovered the well-maintained Bright Angel Trail descending into that incredible beauty, we decided to return the following day for a hike.

It was a pleasant 75 degrees when we left the rim. With the morning coolness and gravity on our side, the six-mile, 3,000-foot descent to our destination at Plateau Point was a relatively easy three-hour hike. Well, what goes down must come up. The temperature at Plateau Point was a searing 103 degrees. With fatigue already a factor, it was clear that the journey back to the rim was not going to be an easy one. After an hour's rest, we started our ascent. A grueling eight hours later we made it to our car.

The hike turned out to be an endurance test that prompted in me a wide range of emotions. I went from being rapt in wonder to borderline despair. I have never been as physically exhausted as I was that evening when we finally emerged from the canyon. In addition to fatigue, I had, for the last several hours, hovered on the verge of heat stroke. Added to these conditions was a knee that decided to act up and deliver excruciating pain with every other step.

Even though my experience in the canyon varied widely, the canyon itself did not change. I went from awestruck in a natural wonderland to near despair, trapped in a seemingly endless trek of pain and suffering. I found it useful to see this experience as a way of understanding why these changes in attitude might occur.

First, the inspiring view drew me in, made me want to plunge into this vast beauty, to interact firsthand with this great canyon. In the early stages of our descent, I marveled at the incomprehensible time it took to form each of the many strata through which we passed. As the day wore on and fatigue and pain set in, I became less focused on our beautiful surroundings and more interested in how much longer we would have to struggle before we finally got out of that fiery furnace. In the beginning I was inspired with the awesome beauty and wonder of this unique place. In the end, because of my lack of conditioning and experience in canyon hiking, I was completely immersed in my body-centered identity and all I cared about was getting to the rim and bringing my suffering to an end.

This latter condition is similar to what happens when you lose the connection with your spiritual essence. Your life becomes a hot and dusty trail that you trudge along, so consumed with physical and mental needs that you forget you are traveling through a spiritual wonderland. In this self-absorbed state, any higher dimension becomes little more than a conceptualized fantasy, a foreign element of little practical value, couched in religious superstition. Your cry for spiritual guidance is a request for directions to the nearest spot of shade or lemonade stand or rescue helicopter or the grand prize of eternal life upon the rim where cool breezes whisper through pines. You wish to be far away from the monotonous drudgery you have been calling life.

If you are looking at your life and asking, "Why am I here?" you might want to consider what you mean by the word *here*. Are you referring to the narrow view of plodding along a hot and dusty uphill trail trying to improve upon or even escape your experience? Or does *here* include the expansive view from the rim, a vast and intriguing panorama that sparks the desire to have a more intimate interaction with this magnificent natural wonder that your life can be? These are two very different responses that are drawn from completely dissimilar visions.

Seeing life as a hot uphill climb causes you to place a high premium on material comforts. When comfort itself becomes an end, it narrows your vision to physical needs and blinds you to the spiritual nature of yourself and your surroundings. If you see life from the wide perspective of the rim, you are going to embrace a much larger view than that prompted by the desire for material comfort. You approach your life more as the early explorer John Wesley Powell did, recording his initial passage through the Grand Canyon. Despite enduring many hardships, this one-armed veteran of the Civil War described the canyon's multicolored strata as "leaves in a great story book."

Many near-death experiencers not only lose their fear of death, they gain a broad perspective of themselves and acquire an even deeper commitment to life. They no longer see their current place on the trail as so much distance from their goal far away upon the rim. They see the trail and their place upon it as an integral part of a vast canyon system. The trail of daily life is not a thing to be escaped but to be lived. Every point along the way offers a uniquely valuable position from which to experience some new aspect of eternity. In other words, their brush with physical death does not alter the trail; it alters their *understanding* of the trail and, more important, it expands their understanding of *themselves*.

If you accept that you have the skills to create a life you are not particularly fond of, then it is not difficult to grasp how using these same skills, but in a slightly different way, can help you get what you want from life. That spiritually enlightened person that you desire to become is within your reach.

Your judgment tells you that if you do something to increase your faith, learn more about creative visualization, and control your will, you can create more desirable material conditions. Consider this: The simple act of worry demonstrates that you are already proficient at using all of these most important creatively influential faculties. When you judge conditions as being negative, you will your imagination to envision an unpleasant scenario. You then substantiate this scenario by letting go of your optimism and turning your faith into all the negative possibilities that might unfold. These become real to you because your executive faculties are fully invested in this perceived scenario.

Suppose you employ these same faculties in a positive way. You decide that some greater good is now evolving out of this appearance. From the positive starting point of inspired judgment, you again will yourself to release your negative imagery and see things working out for your highest good in complete expectation that this improved quality of life is unfolding in greater degrees with each passing day. You can see that in this complete shift of your mind there is nothing new to learn. Do you not already know how to visualize things that are physically absent, or release negative mental and emotional scenarios and infuse your vision with specific expectations? Through the exercise of your will and by using your spiritual discernment to draw from the well of the Infinite, you refocus these familiar faculties in a new and constructive way.

We struggle with the idea that the light of eternity shines only in the now. Imagine standing in the beam of a spotlight whose diameter is six feet. The edge of the light's circle is three feet in every direction from your center. No matter where you go it's always the same. All that you know about your life transpires within this circle. Your past and your future are not in the circle. Past events have left and future events have not arrived. What is within this circle? Your completed soul and its sustaining environment are all that exist here. God, the Creative Life Force, is fully present and active within this circle. You cannot ever become more than you are right now. Your soul is as complete now as it ever will be. Your completeness does not lie outside the circle in a future that you will never reach. Your understanding of God does not depend on more facts that you will accumulate along a future path. You and God are already one. Being one, you already know how to have a relationship. You do not have to learn this. You exist because it is true, it has always been true and there is nothing you can do to change it. You are as close to God as you ever will be. The only thing that needs to occur is a slight shift in perception on your part. Grasp the truth that all you ever can be is now fully present within your circle. Getting what you want from life then becomes a matter of synchronizing your mind with what is true, not someday but now, within your circle.

Getting to this or that place on the trail is not the point. The point is to awaken to who you are, *where* you are and to begin using the faculties you already possess to align yourself with something more than the idea that life is a strenuous uphill battle. All the work you have to do, if you want to call it work, is within your circle of light. The only length of trail you must successfully negotiate is that six-foot diameter that surrounds you. You may think you have to change your conditions or change yourself to make life on earth a more rewarding experience. Because the fullness of God and your completed soul are right where you stand, then the only thing that needs to change is how you think and behave within your eternal circle of light.

The reason you may find it difficult to make this change for the positive is because you are trying to operate outside your circle of light. You might be clinging to failures of the past or trying to correct your entire future before it reaches that three-foot mark in front of you. Attempting to operate outside your circle of light is impossible.

Imagine your soul saying to you:

> Come to me, all you that are weary and are carrying heavy burdens, and I will give you rest. Take my yoke upon you, and learn from me; for I am gentle and humble in heart, and you will find rest for your souls. For my yoke is easy, and my burden is light. (Mt. 11:28-30)

To be gentle and humble in heart is to be in a spiritually receptive state, to draw your attention back into your circle of light where all the life and power and support that you desire already exist. Focus on returning to your center before trying to tackle the whole problem of changing the way you are using your faculties.

In his parable of the talents (Mt. 25:14-30), Jesus tells of a householder who goes on a journey and entrusts his property to his servants. "To one he gave five talents, to another two, to another one, to each according to his ability." Upon returning, the householder praised and advanced the two servants who were given five and two talents, for they invested and doubled their principal amounts. The one who was given one talent buried it because he was afraid of losing it. All three servants were given a thing of value, but only two of them put it to use and were rewarded. The third did not apply what he was given and was punished by his lack of action.

An interesting aspect of this parable is that the householder knew of the three men's abilities even before he distributed the funds. One could argue that he was showing favoritism, that the man given little was destined to fail because life was unfair. In the story, however, the householder decided how much he would give each man according to what he had observed in their previous actions. The one he gave the most was obviously the most industrious. The one he gave the least had been least industrious.

Life does not respond to your shining personality or your good intentions. It responds to the way you employ your executive faculties. If you are pessimistic and fritter away your faith and allow your imagination to run with whatever amuses or consumes you at the moment, you will not build anything of substance. Life does not favor some over others but responds to each according to how they use their faculties. Suppose you had a conversation with God about this. You say, "God, please give me the will to stop doing things I don't want to do. Give me a more positive imagination and deeper faith so I can stop worrying." God would say, "I've given you a perfectly good faculty of will. And you can see that both your imagination and your faith are working quite well. There is nothing I can do when you use your faculties in frivolous pursuits." Had the householder given the most money to the man given the least, the results would have been the same. The man still would have buried the larger amount for fear of losing it.

It is a common error to think that in order to get more of what you want from life you must first acquire new skills, things and conditions that you believe will give you the satisfaction of an awakened soul. When you consciously reconnect with your soul, the light within you comes on. The gloom that plagued you moments earlier is swallowed in the cheering warmth of new inspiration. Your mind bubbles with fresh ideas and a broader, more stable sense of peace and renewed confidence rises from the eternal source of your being. Your material conditions become indicators of needed perceptual changes, stimulating vehicles for unfolding greater aspects of your completed soul. To use the canyon analogy, you shift from the mindset of a hiker struggling to survive a difficult trail to that of the explorer of a great spiritual wonder.

A Personal Challenge

I once found myself in the situation of having my world crumble around me. A professional goal I had set was halted by another person's covert act of deception. The deteriorating situation compounded when people, once friendly and supportive, began to turn hostile. Other former supporters just faded away. It seemed as if every time I prayed for a solution, the opposite would happen. Like Job, all the things I feared fell upon me and I found myself swimming in a raging flood of internal and external negativity. Months passed. Within many of those days I found myself oscillating between unwavering faith and despair. The nights were long and full of demons. I was losing this battle.

Early one morning after yet another fitful night, I went to my usual place of prayer. This time I could not pray for solutions, for I had come to the place where I no longer believed there were any. Mine was an exhausted prayer of total surrender. That morning the light of new strength broke through my consciousness. Nothing on the outside had changed. I had no new ideas about how to fix the situation, but I *knew* everything was going to be fine. I had put my trust in personal powers, in other people, in money. At that moment I rediscovered my true point of strength, my native soul. Though I could not see how, I knew things would work out. In the midst of that tumultuous situation, I found the peace that passes all understanding (Phil. 4:7).

Days passed, and though my world continued its apparent downward spiral, new opportunities slowly appeared and new doors began to open. In time, I emerged into an entirely new world, one that ultimately provided a much better way than I would have considered planning.

That morning in prayer, I did not stop the external turmoil or find a way to get off the hot and dusty trail. I regained the higher vision, the vast view from the rim of the canyon. My faith returned to myself and to my connection with the Infinite. I could once again entertain images of freedom, know a deep sense of peace and feel the cool breezes of a new day full of possibility.

From this higher point of view, I experienced the kind of understanding Joseph must have felt toward his brothers who, out of jealousy, bound and sold him into slavery. He recognized that their evil and self-centered intentions had actually served as the avenue through which a much higher good unfolded to the benefit of all (Gen 50:20). There can be little doubt that through his years of trial Joseph prayed to have his former life and freedom restored. According to the biblical account, this was not to happen, at least not in the way he anticipated. In a later conversation with his brothers, he explained why:

> So it was not you who sent me here, but God; he has made me a father to Pharaoh, and lord of all his house and ruler over all the land of Egypt. (Gen. 45:8)

Joseph's original vision for himself was to start his own family and, like his father, become successful raising livestock in the region of his birth. His life, however, pushed him in another direction.

And so it may be with you. When your best plans begin to unravel and your life spins out of control, your tendency may be to hang on and fight to make things go as your set vision dictates. Such times become an opportunity to re-evaluate your vision, to observe how you are using your faculties and to make sure you are using them from the point of your true strength. Joseph no doubt struggled with each apparently negative development, but we can see that he did not stop just because he was confronted with difficulty. He took each situation and made the most of it. The result was that he found his real and lasting strength, the treasure that remained untouched by moth and rust, safe from the thieves that rob so many of their high vision (Mt. 6:19).

Audio Mixer

To illustrate how our perfectly functional faculties become restricted by our appearance-based vision, we can turn to a piece of electronic equipment known as the audio mixing console. Let's say we have a band of five musicians consisting of three singers, a guitarist and a keyboard player. The group is doing a live performance, so we give each of the three singers a microphone. We plug these microphones, the guitar and the keyboard into individual channels of the console. The volume of each singer and each instrument can now be controlled individually. The band begins to perform and we find singer #2 isn't quite loud enough, so we bring up their volume. The guitar is too loud, so we lower the volume. Now the singers and the instruments sound perfectly balanced, but the overall volume is not quite loud enough. We then turn up a *master volume* that simultaneously brings up all five channels to a suitable level. The master volume, you can see, has a global impact on the entire mix.

Think of your vision as the master volume control and each of your executive faculties—faith, imagination, judgment, will and elimination—as individual channels. The influence that any one of these faculties has on your life will not and cannot exceed the master setting of your vision. If your vision is derived from limited appearances, the exercise of your faith will only affirm and support the restrictions of your appearance-based vision. If you are in communion with your own soul, in touch of your native essence of love, wisdom, life and power, you open the window to the Infinite and your vision becomes charged with spiritual understanding, strength, divine order and the pure energy of enthusiasm.

You do not need to struggle to increase your faith. As your vision expands, your faith will naturally follow. In your quiet times you practice detaching from the many things you are chasing in your mind and you commune with that aspect of yourself that exists above this mental and emotional frenzy. It takes persistence to move into this level of your being, but it is not nearly as difficult as many think. You firmly renounce your need to relive events, manipulate or resolve issues, and allow your soul to detach and rise from the preconceptions and feelings of obligation to roles that do not truly represent you. You are unearthing the hidden treasure of your native soul. Communion with your soul, you understand, is your most valuable asset.

Most of us focus on accomplishing goals without knowing the true reasons why we pursue them. Think of a goal that is important to you and prayerfully consider why you have given it importance. What qualities will the accomplishment of this goal enhance in you? What new powers will it stir? What greater freedom do you believe it will bring? What internal issues do you think it will resolve once accomplished? By asking a few simple questions you quickly see that your goal means more to you than just acquiring a new thing or condition. It involves bringing forth more of what you are at the spiritual level.

Because so many are accustomed to turning to the spiritual side as a means of resolving some external need, few are successful at tapping this higher dimension. They approach their soul with the same motive as one who befriends a person of wealth. They are not interested in actually knowing this person. They think the friendship will benefit them financially. The person of wealth quickly detects their shallow motive.

Likewise, if you approach your soul only with the intention of getting something that will alleviate the suffering of your senses-based identity, it will not show itself in all of its unencumbered state. Your soul shuns the tiny box that your vision has become. At this pristine level, you discover your true source of power and wholeness. Your native soul does not need the patchwork of solutions that you have come up with. You already exist in a condition where all your needs are met and nothing needs to be added. The more you commune with your soul in this quiet and simple way, the broader your vision becomes. Your native strength gradually displaces the weakness of your image-driven personality. You see no need to continue struggling for something you already have. From this point of view, you apply yourself to the opportunities presented in your daily life with freshness and enthusiasm born of your limitless nature. Your growing faith in brighter possibilities unfolding for your life is no longer contrived as a future hope. Your faith in a more expanded life becomes easy and authentic and a daily reality.

You begin to see how clutching at external ideas draws you away from your center of power. This will, in fact, happen many times and you will plunge into some form of misery as a result. Despite these self-imposed wanderings through low and dark periods, you can never damage your native soul. You gradually understand that these eclipsing periods develop when you attempt to derive from people, things and conditions that which you already fully possess. The advent of this inner darkness is only an indication that you are turning away from your source of power, but even in this turning you cannot deplete your perpetually existing resources.

This higher state of being is not something that takes years to develop. Your native soul currently exists in this completed condition. By opening your mind to this all-sufficient level and experiencing firsthand its beauty, power and peace, you develop a consciousness environment that is supportive rather than alien and repelling to your completed soul. Strive to experience this one thing, this conscious union with your fully developed self and you have the spiritual key to getting what you want from life.

Works Cited

Bottorff, J Douglas. *A Practical Guide to Prosperous Living.* West Conshohocken, PA: Infinity Publishing, 2009.

Cady, H. Emilie. *Lessons in Truth.* In *Complete Works of H. Emilie Cady.* Unity Village, MO: Unity Books, 1995.

Eckhart, Meister. *The Essential Sermons, Commentaries, Treatises, and Defense.* Mahwah, NJ: Paulist Press, 1981.

Fillmore, Charles. *The Revealing Word: A Dictionary of Metaphysical Terms.* Unity Village, MO: Unity Books, 1994.

—. *The Twelve Powers.* Unity Village, MO: Unity Books, 2006.

Freeman, James Dillet. *The Story of Unity.* Unity Village, MO: Unity Books, 2007.

Hopkins, Emma Curtis. *High Mysticism.* New York: Cosimo, 2007. Originally published 1888.

Miller, Robert J., ed. *The Complete Gospels.* 4th edition. Salem, OR: Polebridge Press, 2010.

Moody, Raymond. *Life After Life: The Investigation of a Phenomenon—Survival of Bodily Death.* New York: Bantam Books, 1976.

Shanklin, Imelda. *What Are You?* Unity Village, MO: Unity Books, 2005.

Troward, Thomas. *The Doré Lectures on Mental Science.* New York: Dodd, Mead and Company, 1966.

About the Author

J Douglas Bottorff is the author of *A Practical Guide to Meditation and Prayer, A Practical Guide to Prosperous Living*, and *The Whisper of Pialigos*. Ordained in 1981, he has, for nearly three decades, served as minister in churches in Michigan, Missouri and Colorado. He has written extensively for *Unity Magazine*® and is a contributing author to other spiritually based books and periodicals. He has written and recorded two musical CDs, *One World* and *Vision of Hope*. Doug and his wife, Elizabeth, are the parents of two grown children. You may visit his website, *www.jdbottorff.com*, or email him at *jdouglas @jdbottorff.com*.

B0049